# FLESH
# -AND-
# BLOOD
# JESUS

# FLESH -AND- BLOOD JESUS

Learning to Be Fully Human from the Son of Man

## DAN RUSS

BakerBooks

a division of Baker Publishing Group
Grand Rapids, Michigan

Published by Baker Books
a division of Baker Publishing Group
P.O. Box 6287, Grand Rapids, MI 49516-6287
www.bakerbooks.com

Printed in the United States of America

Library of Congress Cataloging-in-Publication Data
Russ, Dan, 1949–
    Flesh-and-blood Jesus : learning to be fully human from the Son of Man / Dan Russ.
        p.   cm.
    Includes bibliographical references.
    ISBN 978-0-8010-6830-0 (pbk.)
    1. Jesus Christ—Example. 2. Jesus Christ—Humanity. 3. Christian life. I. Title.
    BT304.2.R87  2008
    232.9′04—dc22                                                2008002962

To Kathy—
my sister, my bride, and my teacher
(Song of Songs 4:9)

# Contents

# Introduction

## *On Blind Spots and Spotting Blindness*

We often do not see what is staring us in the face. Sometimes we are blind because we refuse to see. My spouse no longer enjoys our time together, but I will not acknowledge that our marriage is failing. Our daughter seems troubled and is losing weight, but we want to believe she is just going through a typical adolescent phase. My father is losing his memory, but I cannot face the prospect of this once-invincible man becoming helpless.

Sometimes, however, we are blind because we have no past experience that would enable us to see what would seem obvious to others. My business partner and lifelong friend is doing questionable deals behind my back. My coach is giving playing time to the teammate whose father bought the team uniforms and subsidized our sports camp this summer. My pastor seems to be working late a lot, causing his administrative assistant to pick her child up late from preschool. Whether we will not see or cannot see, the reality is that most of us have blind spots: the inability to see that which to others in the same situation, or even to us at a later time, is glaringly obvious.

Those who surrounded Jesus were blind, according to the Gospel writers. Of course, we immediately think of the religious leaders who, although eyewitnesses to Jesus's miracles, could only see the fact that he had "worked" on the Sabbath. But what about his followers, many of whom spread palm leaves before him as he entered Jerusalem and then denied and deserted him a week later? Or the eleven, not to mention Judas, who could witness his feeding of thousands and then wonder if he could do it again? What about Peter, who could assert his undying faithfulness, draw a sword in Jesus's defense, and then deny him multiple times, blinded by his own fear? Whether we put on blinders or simply have no lenses to see that which does not fit our experience, we are all prone to impaired vision in our mind's eye.

Sometimes our culture or tradition blinds us. Remember Huck Finn with old Jim, the slave who helped Huck on his journey down the river in Mark Twain's wonderful story. While Huck knows that this gentle man is a human being, his cultural lens causes him to see Jim as a runaway slave, and Huck feels guilty for helping rob a slave owner. Racism is an obvious example, but we can see the same cultural blindness in those of us who can only see the opposite sex, a different ethnicity, another denominational tradition, or folks from another region of our state or country through the lenses of cultural stereotypes and deeply ingrained prejudices.

Jesus understood such blindness among those who witnessed his miracles and heard his teaching. What experience had they with God becoming human, the Messiah inaugurating his kingdom, a prophet performing miracles, or a rabbi who taught like none other they had heard? Jesus knew that only his death and resurrection, followed by the coming of the Holy Spirit, would fully open their eyes, if they chose to see. And this would not be a once-for-all experience. Peter would take years and a second sending of the Holy Spirit to the Gentiles before he would see that the Good News was truly for all people. As the church grew, converts would have to learn these lessons time and again: to accept that Jesus was fully God and fully human and to accept the fact that the Good News of redemption in him was for all people in every dimension of life.

No one better captured this problem of not seeing Jesus fully than Pilate while presiding over Jesus's trial. As you recall, the Jewish leaders brought Jesus to Pilate because they had no authority to put a man to death. Only Roman leaders and Roman law could exact the death penalty. But Pilate had no desire to dirty his hands in this squabble among Jews. On the other hand, he could not afford to offend the high council of Jewish leaders. So he played along, trying to mitigate the situation by interrogating Jesus and permitting his guards to mock and beat him. His hope was that the Jewish leaders would see Pilate as a serious law-and-order ruler and would see Jesus, whom Pilate believed to be innocent, as a beaten and pathetic human being. So Pilate had the guard lead Jesus back into the courtyard of his palace where the Jews awaited his decision. Pilate looked out at them with Jesus standing beside

11

him donned in a purple robe, crowned with thorns, blood running down his swollen face, and declared: "Behold the man!" But these leaders were blind to what Pilate saw—a pathetic, beaten, and innocent human being. They insisted that Pilate crucify him. Pilate was blind to the bloody King of Kings who stood before him. He saw only a pathetic pawn in a political game.

In a sense, like Pilate, those of us who have put our faith in Jesus Christ as the only begotten Son of God, which he most certainly is, are not certain what to make of the fact that he is also the fully human Son of Man, which is expressed so boldly in the words of the Nicene Creed: "For us and for our salvation, he came down from heaven: by the power of the Holy Spirit he became incarnate by the Virgin Mary, and was made man." The creed was written partially in response to various teachings that denied the humanity of Jesus or wanted to split the two natures of Jesus, so that true God and true humanity were not understood as embodied at the same time in Jesus of Nazareth. However, the church, then and now—Protestant, Catholic, and Orthodox—holds that Jesus embodied full divinity and full humanity. While this is the official doctrinal belief of almost all Christians in all times, we still are inclined to see in Jesus the Son of God and to ignore or play down the inseparable truth that he is also the Son of Man.

## The Son of Man

Indeed, the Lord spoke of himself as the Son of Man more than by any other title or designation. Without diminishing the resounding truth that he is the true God, we cannot forget that Jesus speaks of himself as the Son of Man more than eighty times in the Gospels. This title is his chosen title. Interestingly, Jesus is the only one recorded in the Gospels who used this title. Why would he do this, when most of those who doubted or opposed him did so because he was making supernatural claims that no mere man should claim?

Some say that he used this title because it has messianic overtones from the Hebrew Scriptures. The psalmist asks God, "What is man that you are mindful of him, the son of man that you care for him?" (Ps. 8:4). Here the psalmist contrasts the majesty of God with the lowliness of humanity and is mystified that the Sovereign Creator should have crowned the Son of Man with glory. Others have in mind the description of a supernatural presence described in Daniel as "one like a son of man" who comes in the clouds of heaven to receive glory, authority, and sovereign power (Dan. 7:13–14). And the prophet Ezekiel uses it a number of times for those who have the prophetic gift from God. For this reason, we are told by scholars, the followers of Jesus seemed not to question his calling himself the Son of Man, a title familiar to them. While I am sure this is partly true, it does not explain why Jesus uses it of himself more than any other title and why these same followers do not use it at all in the epistles, once he had commissioned them and ascended into heaven.

### Our Surprise vs. God's Surprise

The least we can say is that the title meant more to him than to them. Why? It could be a matter of perspective.

From our perspective, the reality of the Son of God, true God entering our humanity, is astounding, humbling, and mysterious. Most religions, especially those in Greek and Roman cultures, emphasized the chasm between mere mortal humanity and glorious immortal divinity. Even for those steeped in the Jewish tradition, Yahweh is so holy and transcendent, the Creator God of the universe, the King of Kings, that a pious Jew should not write or speak his name. Coming from either of these traditions or, as with many at the time, a confusion of both traditions, we would be astounded that the Son of God should walk with us as the Son of Man.

But if we can presume to imagine the perspective of Jesus, true God and true Man, the astounding, humbling, and mysterious reality for him is to become the Son of Man. Christian teaching is clear that before Jesus of Nazareth was born of Mary, he was in the beginning with the Father and the Spirit, "every single thing was created through, and for, him" and "he is both the first principle and the upholding principle of the whole scheme of creation" (Col. 1:17 Phillips). He created all things with the Father and the Spirit, including humanity, in his image, male and female. But he, to our knowledge, had never in all eternity "made himself nothing, taking the very nature of a servant" (Phil. 2:7) and become flesh: the Son of Man. Theologians and preachers, artists and poets have described, depicted, and portrayed this mystery endlessly, but mostly from the human perspective, trying to fathom the shocking truth that "he came to that which was his own, but his own did not receive him" (John 1:11). And this is shocking. But this is *our* shock, not a surprise to

God, who had been rejected by Israel for centuries. God's shock, if we can imagine such a thing, is to enter into the humanity that God had created millennia before: to be a son of man, to be the Son of Man, to be, in J. B. Phillips's phrase, "supremely human."[1]

## Supremely Human

We can so focus on the realities of our Lord's divinity that we minimize or ignore the realities of his humanity. Even granting its Old Testament messianic overtones, to be the Son of Man meant that Jesus lived humanly in our fallen world, facing our temptations and living out the tensions of being human in the flow of life. He was just like us, human in a sinful world, yet he did not sin.

## So What?

So what can we learn from his glorious life about the meaning of our own humanity, about the tensions of being human in a sinful world and of distinguishing between being a sinner and being a finite flesh-and-blood human being? A few possibilities come to mind.

- We can learn to live gracefully in our bodies, even our wounded and dying bodies.
- We can learn to live with integrity as finite human beings who are created to enjoy limits.
- We can learn to love our family, friends, neighbors, strangers, and enemies.

15

- We can learn to enjoy being alone without being lonely.
- We can learn to enjoy the good things of life: food, feasting, friends, and children, to name a few.
- We can learn to wear our scars with hope and dignity.
- We can learn to die.

In the following pages I invite you to enter into the humanity of Jesus Christ and to allow his humanity to enter you, not as an abstract idea but through the incidents and encounters of his life as he lived it out over thirty-three years and beyond. We will reflect on his life from birth through maturity, suffering, death, and resurrection because that is the way he lived it, like us, one day at a time. We undertake these reflections because he is the way, the truth, and the life—a truly human life. We undertake these reflections because we can only fully embrace Jesus as Lord if we embrace him as the Son of Man as well as the Son of God. And we undertake these reflections because he came to redeem us back to our own humanity.

In the beginning, he was there—God created us as finite human beings and declared us, his image bearers, as the very good consummation of a good creation. After we brought sin into the world, God in Christ entered our fallen world and once again declared our humanity very good. We are being redeemed and will live for eternity as redeemed human beings, not transcendent souls or pious spirits. So we need to get started now, through Christ, to discover how to be finite, embodied reflections of God's grace, even in a sinful world.

## Questions

1. In what ways have you experienced being blind to realities in your life? In what ways has the church or the culture contributed to your blindness?
2. How could Jesus's disciples often be just as blind to who he was as were his enemies?
3. What meanings does the title "the Son of Man" call to your mind?
4. Can you think of examples from the Bible when God seems shocked or surprised?
5. Up to now, what has been your understanding of your belief that Jesus was fully human?

# 1

## Manger Wetter

### *Coming to Terms with Our Neediness*

Wrinkled, Crinkled
Red-skinned Squirmer,
Famished Squealer,
Manger Wetter.
Gabriel salutes you,
Michael bows.
We here in Bethlehem
Bed you with cows.
We here in Bethlehem
Bed you with cows.

Stephen Mahan[1]

When we reflect on the humanity of Jesus, our minds most easily leap to Jesus the mature man. This leap is understandable, since most of the four Gospels focus on the adult ministry, teachings, miracles, relationships, suffering, death, and resurrection of the Lord. Only Matthew and Luke record accounts of his birth and a glimpse of his childhood.

What does it mean that Jesus began dwelling among us as baby flesh? This question troubled many of the early church fathers, some of whom tried to deny that Jesus was truly God and truly human. Some were particularly repelled at the idea and the image of the Second Person of the Trinity entering the world through a woman's womb. But this ancient heresy, sometimes attributed to Nestorius, is not merely ancient, as I discovered some years ago. As the headmaster of a Christian school, I sent out a yearly Christmas card. One year the poem on the card was "Manger Wetter," the text of which opens this chapter. While most responses I received were very positive and polite, to my surprise I received a few stinging letters of rebuke, all from older, biblically literate, ostensibly mature Christian leaders. The general sentiment was that the poet, a friend and Lutheran pastor, and I had committed sacrilege by suggesting that the Lord Jesus Christ was a "manger wetter." I was stunned to realize how these pious Christians were repulsed by the truth that Jesus "was made man," beginning like all humanity as a baby. They could not imagine that he had truly entered humanity, and, I suspect, they were repulsed in the depths of their hearts by the realities of their own humanity.

What is it that repulses us about God being a manger wetter? Some of us were taught not to discuss, better yet not to think about, the fact that human beings pass some of the food and drink they consume. We are taught that to discuss such topics is vulgar and dirty. Therefore, we infer that the realities themselves are vulgar and dirty. Nor do people who talk openly about such things help much, since so many of them speak of passing food, water, and gas as something hilariously dirty. Finally, the idea that any of us, much less God, should wet the bed means we are not in control, and who can imagine God not being in control of everything?

## The Beauty of Baby Flesh

Over the centuries, Christian artists have probably more readily embraced the mystery of God becoming baby flesh than have many Christian theologians. The very paradox that puzzles or repels some pietistic Christian thinkers intrigues and attracts Christian artists. For example, John Donne is one of many Christian poets who embrace the mystery of God as infant and never more powerfully than in the second poem of his seven-sonnet cycle entitled "Annunciation":

> Salvation to all that will is nigh;
> That All, which always is all everywhere,
> Which cannot sin, and yet all sins must bear,
> Which cannot die, yet cannot choose but die,
> Lo! faithful Virgin, yields Himself to lie
> In prison, in thy womb; and though He there
> Can take no sin, nor thou give, yet He'll wear,
> Taken from thence, flesh, which death's force may
>     try.
> Ere by the spheres time was created, thou
> Wast in His mind, who is thy Son, and Brother;
> Whom thou conceives't, conceiv'd; yea thou art
>     now

21

Thy Maker's maker, and thy Father's mother;
Thou hast light in dark, and shutt'st in little room,
Immensity cloister'd in thy dear womb. [2]

The poem captures the absurdity of the omnipotent, omniscient, omnipresent, and holy God condescending into Mary's womb, choosing her to become her "Maker's maker" and her "Father's mother." Rather than moving beyond the literal facts of his incarnation, the poem contemplates the meaning of God as fetus, as flesh, as finite.

In rendering and reflecting on the concrete reality of Jesus's infant humanity, artists like Donne carry on the bold tradition of biblical writers. Isaiah, in what Christians take to be a messianic prophecy, describes a world in desperate need of a savior who can redeem the people from the clutches of bloody tyrants:

> The people walking in darkness
>     have seen a great light,
> on those living in the land of the shadow of death
>     a light has dawned. . . .
> Every warrior's boot used in battle
>     and every garment rolled in blood
> will be destined for burning,
>     will be fuel for the fire.
> For to us a child is born,
>     to us a son is given,
>         and the government will be on his shoulders.
>
> Isaiah 9:2, 5–6

How shocking to follow the images of warriors' boots and garments rolled in blood with "For to us a child is born"! One expects that following such striking images of bloody warfare the prophet would give us the image of Messiah as righteous warrior, as judge, an Achilles or Ben Hur. But instead he describes the hope of Israel as first a child, a son. And old Simeon continues with this prophetic imagination when the Gospel of Luke describes this old flesh taking this young infant into his arms, looking the baby in the eye and, instead of cooing, declaring, "My eyes have seen your salvation, which you have prepared in the sight of all people, a light for revelation to the Gentiles, and for glory to your people Israel" (2:30–32). He then turns to Mary and Joseph, who marvel at his words, and says, "This child is destined to cause the falling and rising of many in Israel" (2:34). As this exchange is carried on among them, Jesus, we can imagine, is sleeping or looking about him, or even crying. But this does not prevent these adult Jews from seeing in this infant the hope of Israel and the entire world.

By contrast, other stories of miraculous births that were thick in the air when Jesus walked the earth tend toward the miracle child either being born an adult or being born a baby with miraculous powers. An example of the first is the story of the birth of Athena, the Greek goddess of wisdom. She is born from the forehead of her father, Zeus, full of wisdom and divinity. A variation of the birth of a miracle-working child is found in the *Mwindo Epic*, a story of the Nyanga people of the Democratic Republic of Congo. Mwindo, whose name means "the little one just born he walks," is the child of a tribal chief, Shemwindo. The chief has sworn that he will not let a male child live, because that child would be his successor and remind him of his mortality. So the gods give Mwindo special powers, even in the womb, to escape his father's attempts to kill him and to defeat his father in battle. While this is a unique expression of heroic literature, it is a typical description of a child born as a demigod or with miraculous gifts from the gods.[3] Such miracle babies are almost never described as normal babies, as was Jesus. I suspect this is because most religions and myths cannot comprehend true divinity becoming true humanity or because they have such disdain for "the human condition" that they prefer their heroes to be all-powerful from the start. Jesus, by contrast, entered helpless humanity helpless, as real babies really do.

### Weak and Needy

So what does the helpless infant humanity of Jesus imply about our humanity?

First, Jesus, especially in infancy but not only as an infant, was weak and needy. He had to rely on Mary and Joseph, as well as other adults in his extended family, to feed, wipe, and hold him, and until a certain age he could only communicate that need by crying. To be weak and needy, powerless to manage some of life's problems and challenges in one's own strength, is to be human—not a sin. We will discuss later some other incidents when Jesus was weak and needy—after fasting in the desert, when seeking solitude to pray, and in the Garden of Gethsemane, to name a few. For now, let it suffice to say that our Lord was weak and needy, yet without sin, which raises the question of how we can be the same.

Accepting weakness and need is perhaps more difficult for modern Americans than for most people in the history of the world. While all human beings wrestle with pride— thinking more highly of themselves than they ought—we Americans place a very high value on being "self-made," independent, and not reliant on or a burden to anyone. While this is not necessarily the freedom described by the founding fathers (for life, liberty, and the pursuit of happiness are all perfectly possible for people who know they are weak and needy), early in the American story we envisioned freedom as autonomy. Founders such as Benjamin Franklin, novelists such as James Fenimore Cooper, poets such as Walt Whitman, along with a wide array of folk heroes and industrial giants, wove into the American myth that freedom and the pursuit of happiness meant making one's way in the world without asking anyone for anything. Indeed, to be weak and needy in our culture is shameful.

Of course there are those in the contemporary world wise enough to realize that not acknowledging weakness and need does not lead to freedom and happiness. For those who have found healing and redemption in Alcoholics Anonymous or other recovery groups, acknowledging weakness and need is the alpha and omega of healthy freedom. But admitting such limits is also important for those who, far from struggling with addictions, are leaders in business, politics, and other professions. No less a thinker than the late Peter Drucker, grandfather of the modern principles of business management, has written that all organizations are based on human strengths and weaknesses. According to Drucker, organizations exist because every human being, no matter how gifted, has strengths and weaknesses. "So we organize in order to maximize our strengths and to minimize our weaknesses."[4]

In other words, all human beings are strong and weak, adequate and needy. Wise people, honest people are willing to acknowledge both, understanding that weaknesses are nothing to be ashamed of. Rather, they witness to the God-given limits of physical size, age, gifts, skills, and personal inclinations. To take a common example, having a "weakness for chocolate" should simply mean that a person loves to eat one of the most delectable treats that God enabled humans to create. Giving our lives over to such a "weakness" to the detriment of our health is a sin, but psychologists would agree that such an unhealthy obsession has nothing to do with the joy of eating a tasty food. And yet there is a tradition from ancient to modern ascetics that would have us deny and never indulge our weakness or need for anything.

### Ignorant Like Jesus

Jesus was also ignorant as a baby. We are accustomed to referring to God as omniscient, and I have no interest in debunking such a doctrine, but I wonder what meaning "omniscience" has in the case of a baby who in every other way was very much a baby. Do we really want to assert that this baby, though God incarnate, understood in his babyness how all the cosmos came into being? Did Mary never teach him anything, because he knew it all? This is silly; it defies common sense as well as the Gospel stories. So we are left to believe that Jesus was indeed a baby, much as you and I were once babies with so much to learn.

While his knowledge was limited even as a mature adult, we cannot escape his limited knowledge when a baby. We all accept and celebrate the ignorance of babies, because one of the delights of helping them grow is to witness their constant learning. They begin by knowing little more than their own needs and comforts, crying and cooing for whoever will feed, change, and hold them. Quickly they discover that the people who care for them are specific people: Mom and Dad. The rest of the world is, at first, not-Mom and not-Dad. Though we begin our lives in ignorance, eventually the very reality of being ignorant—not knowing—soon becomes an embarrassment to us, a limit of which we are ashamed and want to hide. But not Jesus. He knew, as a human, that he did not and need not know everything.

Satan, by contrast, is a know-it-all, brilliantly described by John Milton in his masterwork, *Paradise Lost*. When Satan selects himself to scout out God's new creation, where it is rumored that God has made creatures for whom he has a deep love, Satan must travel from hell to earth through space. C. S. Lewis points out in his *Preface to Paradise Lost* that everything Satan sees reminds him of himself: how he feels, what he thinks, what he covets, and what he lost. In other words, everything exists for him and about him. This reduction of the whole world to his ego-centric understanding of reality enabled him to maintain the illusion of being omniscient. Adam, on the other hand, loves to find out about creation, both on earth and in the heavenlies, precisely because he knows that they are mysteriously different from him, and he longs to understand something of their mystery. Before Adam sins, God sends

27

the angel Raphael to instruct Adam, and Adam's desire is to know more about everything else in God's creation, indeed to lose himself and his self-consciousness in learning. Adam is not the expert who must pretend to know everything; he is the amateur who genuinely longs to learn so that he can better love.[5]

### The Freedom of "I Don't Know"

This contrast between a self-centered perspective that would master and consume everything into itself and an other-centered perspective that would seek to understand and love everything brings to mind Peter Senge's critique of our modern obsession with expertise. Senge, who advocates "learning organizations" where people are motivated to continually and freely share knowledge, says that organizations, including academic institutions, are instead preoccupied with expertise. Experts are, by definition, people who know the answers about a given, usually very narrow, piece of knowledge, which they do not share freely because their security and prosperity are based on controlling that knowledge. And they never admit to ignorance, so no real learning can take place in such a community.[6]

I suspect that the reason we are tempted to think of ignorance—limits to our knowledge—as shameful, if not sinful, is that our minds have seemingly unlimited limited capacity to know more and more, unlike our bodies, which have definite limits. By unlimited limited capacity, I mean that while our bodies can only be one place at a time, our minds can wander in the past and future, here and there, contemplating this and that while our bodies are sitting in a chair. The mind seems more godlike than the body, although still finite and limited, because it gives us the illusion of not being bound by time or space.

Jesus, beginning in infancy, sinlessly embodied and later embraced the limits of human knowledge. Even in his messianic manhood he freely, without shame or guilt, replied to his disciples' question about when the final judgment would occur that "no one knows about that day or hour . . . only the Father" (Matt. 24:36). Indeed, James Fowler in his insightful book *Becoming Adult, Becoming Christian* says that one of the freedoms God calls us to is to discover and celebrate the unique ways God has gifted each of us. In doing so, we enter an "ecology of giftedness" where "we are freed from either the inflation of trying to be Godlike in super—or omni—competence or the deflation that inevitably comes when we fail and find our limits." He concludes, "We can experience our limits as gracious, even as we can experience our gifts as gracious."[7] We are, in short, created with limited ways and abilities to know the world, so that we may enjoy needing God and each other.

### The Hope in Need

Finally, we can discover in Jesus and his parents the power of hope in the reality of weakness and need. When Jesus was born, Mary, Joseph, and a handful of others knew that this child was the hope for Israel and the world. Against common sense and ruthless opposition they trusted God's leading and protection with that hope in mind. Just as Jesus grew in knowledge and wisdom, he must have grown in hope. From the cradle he learned to hope that crying would bring his mother to feed him and that his neediness would cause Joseph to protect and provide for him. For hope is that deep assurance that more is yet to come, in physical growth and sustenance, in knowledge and wisdom, and in love.

## Questions

1. What do you imagine Jesus was like as a baby?
2. Why do you think God did not become a miracle baby, like so many of the mythic heroes, doing mighty deeds from the womb?
3. How do you struggle with being weak and needy?
4. Why is it so hard, even shameful, for us to confess our ignorance?
5. Have you ever experienced freedom in saying, "I don't know; teach me"?

# 2

## Longing to Belong

### *Finding Our Place in the World*

"Nazareth! Can anything good come from there?"
Nathaniel asked.

John 1:46

Jesus's baby-fleshed humanity reminds us that to be human is to be finite, and that to be limited is not sin. We were created in time and space for time and space, not in eternity and infinity. Our finite bodies can only be present one place at a time, one second at a time. To be born in this time and in this place is God-given and Christ-affirmed, whether that is in first-century Bethlehem or in twenty-first-century Madisonville. While we also have the God-given capacity to think of and imagine other places and other times, we must do so from the limits of our embodied place and our given time. To long to escape my body, my place, and my time is to participate in the sin of Adam and Eve, who rejected their finite humanity. This longing not to be ourselves is common to all of us. I remember looking at Charles Atlas bodybuilding ads in my comic books and wanting to look like that, not like me. Likewise, in a nation of industrial gypsies, I share in that economic and psychological illusion that I can move out and move up and start a brand new life. Finally, we all participate in that dream of a time machine that could take us back to a better time in our own lives, if not a better time in history, or forward to a fantastic future.

### Unique People, Places, and Times

Jesus did not attempt to escape his body, his place, and his time. Born in Bethlehem, exiled to Egypt, coming to maturity in Nazareth, and ministering in Galilee and Judea, he could only live, preach, heal, and pray in one place, one day at a time. His life can teach us to live with our limits as a gift from God.

Indeed, the Bible is striking in its constant references to people, places, and times. The Hebrew and Christian Scriptures have none of that fairytale language: "Once upon a time in a far-off land." The creation narrative in Genesis may be perceived that way with its startling opening, "In the beginning, God created . . ." but then it goes on to say what God created and in what order, with trees that bear fruit that contains seeds that produce trees, and all of this happening in a place called Eden where four rivers—including the Tigris and Euphrates—run through it. This cataloguing of definite people, places, and times in the first couple of chapters does not stop there. It continues throughout Genesis, the other books of Moses, and the rest of the Old Testament. Individual people, particular places, and historic moments matter.

Likewise, the New Testament participates in this Jewish emphasis on the definite by telling the reader that Jesus was born in Bethlehem of Judea when particular Roman and Jewish rulers were in power, that his family fled to Egypt until Herod died, and that they returned to Nazareth, where Jesus grew to maturity. Why this relentless, strange, even tedious emphasis on place? It forces many readers of the Bible to refer to maps and footnotes to know where in the world is being described and has led countless people of faith to go on pilgrimages to walk where Abraham and Sarah, Moses, Aaron, and Miriam, David, Jesus, Mary, and the apostles once walked. However, it motivates some readers to gloss over these details and concern themselves with the "spiritual level" of the biblical texts.

But the biblical writings will have none of this truth beyond the literal; truth is found in and through the reality of things, because God created real people with finite bodies to live in real places and in time, from the beginning. God chose to redeem the world by making, through Abram and Sarai, a nation, a unique and particular people who would bless all the other unique and particular peoples of the earth. He sent individual judges and kings to lead the people in places and times of crisis. Eventually, in the fullness of time, God became flesh through the body of Mary, who bore the child in Bethlehem and who with her husband Joseph fled to Egypt, and who all returned to

Nazareth in Galilee. To some high-minded thinkers it seems scandalous that Christians should believe that the Creator of all things could become one of the things he created in an obscure place like Nazareth. After all, even Nathaniel, a disciple of Jesus, posed the question, "What good thing can come from Nazareth?"

## A New Sense of Place

In his birth, his family's flight to Egypt, and their eventual home-making in Nazareth, Jesus affirmed the human significance of having a place, knowing our place, leaving our place, losing our place, and recovering a new sense of place. Being finite and limited creatures, we are created to inhabit particular places that will define to some extent who we are long before we can redefine either that place or ourselves. Places do, in truth, shape our character and calling. To be from Nazareth or Chicago affords a perspective on the world that is unique; this is not to say that the world is totally different depending on where we are from, but it is to say that we view the world from different angles depending on where we live.

Most large cities throb with diverse people and cultures, with the energy that such diversity creates. But we seldom know many of those people as persons. The small Galilean or the modern New England village affords all the comfort of familiarity, simplicity, and quaintness. We know virtually all of the townsfolk and they us, sometimes too well. Unlike so many of us, Jesus was never ashamed of where he grew up, even though it was no place of honor among the Jews and Gentiles of his time. Not only, to our knowledge, did he spend most of his thirty-three years there, he also carried on much of his public ministry in the region where he grew up, not, as one might expect, in and around Jerusalem. Perhaps he knew, as many scholars suggest, that traveling in and around Jerusalem would lead quickly to confrontation with the Jewish leaders and to his death. He might have chosen to avoid the holy city until it was time to fulfill his calling. But I think we can also surmise that he savored being near home for as long as possible, because what could he possibly find in Jerusalem and Judea that he could not find in Nazareth and Galilee, including most of his apostles? He had known early in his life what it was like to be displaced, when his family fled to Egypt, and he probably did not like the feeling.

### Truth Everywhere

Jesus of Nazareth, born in Bethlehem, died, buried and resurrected in Jerusalem, became flesh, grew to maturity, lived and ministered in real places. From the places he dwelt we learn something about our places and all places in creation. First, we learn that truth is found every place. The one who said, "I am the way, the truth, and the life" was truth in Bethlehem, in Egypt, in Nazareth, and in Jerusalem, not to mention the countless towns and villages he journeyed through in his brief life. While Jerusalem was and is sacred to Jews and now Christians, it is not because one must go there to find the truth, as exiled Jews have discovered. The "heavens declare the glory of God" every place. God made places and made us to dwell in places, but truth knows no limits—it can find us out; we can discover it anywhere.

## Goodness in All Places

Likewise, every place is a good place; goodness is boundless and can be experienced among people who embody it in countless places. Now this is not the way most people think, then or now. Most people believe that to be from their place is good, but you can't trust "those people over there." To the Jews it was the Egyptians, to the Egyptians it was nomads, to the Greeks it was the barbarians, to the Romans it was the Goths, to the English it was the French, and so forth. We handily categorize the good humans and the bad humans by place. Where my mother grew up in Muhlenberg County, Kentucky, "you couldn't trust anyone from Grayson County." Where our children grew up in North Texas, we all knew "what kind of people come out of the Big Thicket in East Texas." Where we live now, near Boston, you know there will be trouble when people move in from Lynn or Lowell, and let's not even discuss those bizarre people from certain parts of Maine.

The Scriptures will have none of this geographical fatalism that dismisses individuals, families, towns, and whole ethnic groups on the basis of "what good thing can come out of _____?" Indeed, as ruthless and evil as certain generations of Egyptians and Babylonians were to ancient Hebrews, the vision God gives Isaiah of "that day" when his kingdom will be fulfilled, describes a time when nations once locked in a deadly game of mutual destruction will love their neighbors as themselves:

In that day there will be a highway from Egypt to Assyria. The Assyrians will go to Egypt and the Egyptians to Assyria. The Egyptians and Assyrians will worship together.

36

In that day Israel will be the third, along with Egypt and Assyria, a blessing on the earth. The LORD Almighty will bless them, saying, "Blessed be Egypt my people, Assyria my handiwork, and Israel my inheritance."

19:23–25

God's goodness and God's good people can be found anyplace where people accept his grace, worship like the Egyptians and the Assyrians will do, and bless all the motley peoples and places on God's good earth.

## Beauty All Over the Place

Finally, Jesus of Nazareth reminds us of the beauty of each place and of all places. One of the startling characteristics of the Old Testament is that while God gave the descendants of Abraham a Promised Land, God did so as the Creator of all lands, all places, and through Israel, as the one who seeks to bless all the nations of the earth. There are no ugly places, except where humanity has marked them with sin and suffering. But even when this occurs, the beauty of God's presence can break through, as Gerard Manley Hopkins renders in his poem about the fallen glory of creation:

### "God's Grandeur"

The world is charged with the grandeur of God.
It will flame out, like shining from shook foil;
It gathers to a greatness, like the ooze of oil
Crushed. Why do men then now not reck [take
     heed] his rod?
Generations have trod, have trod, have trod;

And all is seared with trade; bleared, smeared with
toil;
And wears man's smudge and shares man's smell:
the soil
Is bare now, nor can foot feel, being shod.

And for all this, nature is never spent;
There lives the dearest freshness deep down things;
And though the last lights off the black West went
Oh, morning, at the brown brink eastward,
springs—
Because the Holy Ghost over the bent
World broods with warm breast and with ah!
bright wings.[1]

This is not a romantic view of the ways human beings
have abused the places we have been given. Hopkins's images are those of generations trodding and trading the
earth and her treasures, dirtying her beauty and causing
her to stink with their sinful nature. Nevertheless, "nature
is never spent."

## Jesus in Our Places

We all need a place to be loved, nurtured, and protected.
From the cradle in the apartment or house where we are
born to the bed in the house or hospice where we will pass
on to his presence, we need our places. We need to belong to
real families, neighborhoods, churches, and communities.
Human beings have entertained fantasies of transcending
place for many centuries. In Eastern religions and philosophies, that fantasy takes the form of reincarnation or other

forms of escaping not only a given place but also finally the annihilation of the self. In the humanistic religions and philosophies of the West, the fantasy of transcending place can either be a Platonic ideal—living in our heads as if to transcend time and space and pre-existing and being beyond time and space—or, more commonly, being a cosmopolitan. The latter fantasy of utopia is to identify with a "world class" city or culture, which is every place and needs no other place; ancient versions are Babylon, Alexandria, Athens, and Rome; modern versions are New York, Paris, London, or Tokyo.

When we add contemporary technologies to these illusions, we believe that we can stand in these great cities and, through cell phone, computer, and iPod, be omnipresent, if not omnipotent and omniscient. In other words, while our finite bodies are moving about these modern Babels, we do so absentminded, absent-souled, and absent a real place in the world. This is the opposite of Jesus of Nazareth, who knew where he was from and where he was going, and was present everyplace he journeyed in the meantime.

We cannot forget that Jesus of Nazareth was first Jesus of Bethlehem and Jesus of Egypt—a displaced person. We can be displaced providentially (Joseph and Mary went to Bethlehem to fulfill the Roman census), by violence (they fled Herod's heinous attempt to murder the one born "King of the Jews"), or by following God's guidance (they chose a place far away from Jerusalem to raise the Christ child). No matter why we are displaced, losing home is painful, confusing, and exhilarating. The pain of displacement comes from losing familiar people, smells, furniture, streets, neighbors, stores, restaurants, shops, doctors, mechanics, trees, birds, languages, and accents. These common presences are lost to us, whether we are political refugees, as are so many in our broken world, or industrial gypsies taking a job offer in a strange city. In a world where hundreds of millions of people have been displaced by war, famine, oppression, poverty, natural disasters, and opportunity, it is helpful to remember Jesus too was a displaced person. Jesus of Nazareth understood from the beginning to the end of his life what it means to be displaced, by violence, by choice, and by calling.

## A Final Place

Jesus does not call us to utopian dreams of idealized places—suburbs, Disney Worlds, planned communities, virtual fantasies—but to the places and the dis-places where he and the truth, goodness, and beauty of creation are present and real. When he was trying to teach his apostles on the night he was betrayed, we are told that he retreated to "the upper room" in Jerusalem where they ate and worshiped, and where he told them what was to come. He was about to leave them; they were disoriented and, frankly, frightened. He did not tell them of transcending truths and utopian visions. He said, "In my Father's house are many rooms; if it were not so, I would have told you. I am going there to prepare a place for you. And if I go and prepare a place for you, I will come back and take you to be with me that you also may be where I am" (John 14:2–3). In other words, the vision that Jesus of Nazareth gives of heaven is of a place where there is room for everyone.

## Questions

1. What do you make of the fact that Jesus is born in Bethlehem, outside of Jerusalem, and grows up in Egypt and Nazareth?
2. In what ways did people then and now perceive Jesus because of his provincial upbringing?
3. How do you think spending his early years in Egypt, probably in a Jewish district of a city, influenced Jesus as a child?
4. Do you find yourself thinking of certain cities or regions as smart, good, and beautiful and others as backward, sinister, and ugly? What is your response when you meet people from "those places"? Are you from one of those places of which people ask, "What good thing can come from there?" How does that make you feel?
5. In what ways do you and people you know feel like displaced persons? How can Jesus's displaced life and promise of a room for each of us help us recover a sense of belonging now?

# 3

## Mother's Guilt

### *Living in the Tension Between a Parent's Will and God's Will*

> When your mother asks, "Do you want a piece of advice?" it's a mere formality. It doesn't matter if you answer yes or no. You're going to get it anyway.
>
> Erma Bombeck[1]

Erma Bombeck addresses one of the great tensions of Jesus's life and, for that matter, one of the great tensions faced by all human beings. How do you respond to the woman who risked her life to bring you into the world, who wants the best for you, and who does not seem to understand who you are called to be? In Jesus's case, the dilemma was even more complicated by the fact that his mother is called highly favored, blessed among women, and the obedient servant of God. If Bombeck is right in her definition of guilt, "the gift that keeps on giving," then no one can push those buttons like Mother, even if she does not intend to do so. All of us with mothers who have loved us have felt that sense of failure that we are not living up to her expectations, whether or not she has ever expressed her expectations for our lives. The relationship between mothers and children, especially "good mothers" and children, is a mystery. And no such relationship has ever been portrayed by artists, poets, and theologians more than that of Madonna and Child.

Two revealing episodes from the New Testament describe how Jesus related to his mother, especially when she volunteered unsolicited advice and expectations. The first was when he was twelve years old and journeyed with his parents to the Feast of the Passover. The second was when he was thirty years old and attended a wedding in the town of Cana. Each took place at a crossroads in the life of Jesus. At the first crossroads, Jesus was a Jewish boy of twelve beginning his preparation for bar mitzvah, when he would officially enter adulthood. The second was when Jesus, at thirty, could enter into public ministry as a rabbi. Interestingly, each of these events takes place at a celebration: the Feast of Passover and the wedding at Cana. We cannot forget that in most of the ancient world, males and females did not mix much, except as families in the home. So when there is opportunity for parents and children to spend extended time together, as with most holidays, tensions can run high. What can we learn from each experience in Jesus's life that might inform our relationships with parents in general and mothers in particular?

43

## Do You Not Understand?

We recall from Luke's account (Luke 2:22–52) that Mary and Joseph are leaving Jerusalem following Passover and have traveled a day before realizing Jesus is missing. Since Jewish pilgrims caravanned together to the great feasts, it is easy to understand how Mary and Joseph presume that Jesus is traveling and playing with extended family or neighbors. Teachers of Scripture have enjoyed many laughs imagining what it felt like to lose the Messiah. The panic that any parent feels when he or she realizes that a child is missing must have been magnified beyond our comprehension. Losing Jesus was, for them, both losing their own child and a child entrusted to their care by the Almighty Father.

They take a day to return to Jerusalem, where they find Jesus at the temple "sitting among the teachers, listening to them and asking them questions." In normal circumstances this would arouse a shock of delight and pride in parents of a twelve-year-old. But this was neither a normal circumstance nor a normal twelve-year-old. Mary may have spoken in anger, frustration, hurt, or all three; she could not understand how this boy of all boys could have "treated us like this." After all, he was born to her, a virgin, by the power of the Holy Spirit. She, Zechariah, Simeon, and Anna had prophesied about this child "who will be called a prophet of the Most High" and "a light for revelation to the Gentiles and for glory to your people Israel." How could he, who could dialogue with Israel's wisest teachers, not understand the fear and anxiety he had caused Mary and Joseph?

The reply of Jesus is the reply of a kid who is also God: "Why were you searching for me?" he asked. "Didn't you know I had to be in my Father's house?" Unless we believe that he is asking a rhetorical question—the story does not indicate that he is—we are listening to the naïve voice of the sinless boy-son of God who genuinely does not understand why his parents do not understand his motivations and actions. He seems truly puzzled at Mary's rather accusatory question and her wounded tone of voice. He is undoubtedly wise beyond any boy who ever walked the earth, but here he is truly a boy. We are told, "Then he went down to Nazareth with them and was obedient to them." Luke frames this whole episode with the prescript and postscript "that Jesus grew in wisdom and stature, and in favor with God and man."

### The Mystery of Others

Jesus was God, yes. But he was human, and humans do not know everything. We do not know fully what we know. And we do not know what we do not know. Jesus participated in this finite humanity, this inability to know the thoughts, motivations, and feelings of others, even his parents, perhaps especially his parents, who had nursed, played with, cleaned, and changed the diapers of this mortal baby who was also the Son of God.

This incident reveals much about being human, even a sinless human in a fallen world. It reminds us how we do not understand each other because we are finite, by God's design, and because we are individuals, also by God's design. Jesus reminds us that a child must learn what his parents want, need, expect, think, and feel; likewise, parents must learn the same of their children. This does not come automatically. One has to grow in such wisdom through mistakes. Only love and trust prevent such mistakes from deteriorating into sinful attitudes, words, and actions. Jesus knew that Mary and Joseph loved him, and he knew his Father commanded that he honor them. So he entrusted himself to them and grew. They loved him, and I'm certain they too grew in wisdom and favor with God.

## Do You Still Not Understand?

It might seem, according to Luke's narrative, that the holy family moved forward without having to revisit this tension again. Fast-forward eighteen years. Jesus is thirty, and Mary is, to the best of our knowledge, around forty-five years old. Jesus and some of his disciples accompany his mother to a wedding in the obscure town of Cana. Jesus has already begun his public ministry as a rabbi and called his first disciples. He is in every respect a mature human being and fully conscious of his messianic calling.

The description of the encounter between Mary and Jesus is cryptic but telling (John 2:1–11). John simply writes that when the wine was gone—an embarrassment to the hosts—Mary looks at Jesus and says, "They have no more wine." That could be taken as a statement of fact, a whisper of scandal, or an expression of pity, except that Jesus does not hear it any of these ways. We may assume that Mary's tone and the way she looks at Jesus indicates that she is expecting, even commanding, Jesus to do something about this. For he instantly counters, "Dear woman, why do you involve me?" He then explains, "My time has not yet come." He does not ask, "Mother, how may I help?"

or assure her "Don't worry, I will take care of it." Even if we read the tone of his response as good-humored, spoken by a son who banters back and forth with a mother who is always telling him what to do, we cannot avoid hearing at least a gentle scold in his words.

Mary ignores both his words and the tone of his voice. She simply turns to the servants with supreme confidence and says, "Do whatever he tells you." You know the rest of the story. Jesus honors his mother's concern and presumption, the wedding hosts are spared embarrassment, the best wine is shared by all, and Jesus does the first of his miraculous signs. As the old joke goes, "My mother knows how to push all my buttons. She should; she installed them."

A friend of mine, who is about forty years old, complains, "Every time I visit my mother, she greets me by checking my forehead for fever!" It works both ways, doesn't it? Not only can Mother not help mothering even an adult child, but many of us adults slip back into childish behavior in the presence of our mothers. The least this tells us is that there is a profound bond between mother and child, one that not even the sinless Son of God could escape. Since Jesus does not denounce Mary's attitude and words in either situation as sinful or self-centered—he does not hesitate to rebuke her later, when she and his brothers try to force him to go home (Mark 3:20–35)—we assume that she is responding to her son in a way that reflects God's design for familial love. Since we believe that the Lord lived a perfectly human life, tempted in every way as we are and yet without sin, we assume that his honest, puzzled, reproachful, and respectful responses were fully human and sinless.

### Embracing the Tensions of Loving Parents

So what do these encounters of Jesus with his mother tell us about our own humanity? First, they indicate that feeling tension between a mother's best wishes for her child and the child's personal sense of calling is perfectly normal. Both mother and child must spend a lifetime learning to know, respect, honor, and love one another. Understanding must come through respectful and loving misunderstanding. As the Greek chorus in Sophocles's tragedy *Antigone* declares: "We must suffer into truth." Even the God/Man, to be fully human, suffered into truth. And there are several truths that Mary and Jesus suffered into. First, loving another, even a parent or a child, does not mean we understand the other. In a sense, we can never understand another person fully. Otherwise, individuality would not exist. We could be like that primordial Greek goddess of the earth, Gaia, who was said to give life to her children and then swallow them back into herself. More specifically, the command to honor our parents all the days of our lives does not mean that we obey their will for us all the days of their lives. There comes a time when we are called by God "to leave father and mother," whether that be to cleave to a spouse and start a new family or to follow a call to a life that is God's vocation for us and not necessarily the dream our parents have for us. Finally, having loving respect for others does not mean we fully understand them nor does loving respect for parents mean that we obey their plans for us all of our lives. We must accept the reality that relating to one another in loving respect is a lifetime project. We do not fully master this loving tension. And why should we, if our Lord did not?

### Mother or Smother?

I conclude by suggesting that there is a creative as well as destructive dimension of the mother/child relationship. The biblical narratives are replete with the stories of powerful mothers who mentor or smother their sons. Sarah protects Isaac from the usurpation that Hagar and Ishmael conspire to do. Rebekah enables Jacob to deceive his father and steal Esau's blessing from old Isaac. Hannah asks God for a child, and when God blesses her with Samuel, she dedicates the child to serve God the rest of his life. Bathsheba conspires to obtain David's anointing of Solomon as his successor. In other words, for good or ill, sometimes for both, the power of mothers and of the maternal in the lives of individuals and cultures cannot be overestimated and must be reckoned with.

Jesus's relationship with Mary enables us to accept the humanity of this wonderful, loving, difficult, and lifelong tension that enables a mother and son, a parent and child to grow through grace to embrace one another through and beyond the biological, to honor and love one another even when we must ask the perennial question, "Do you not yet understand?"

### Questions

1. What do you imagine it was like for Mary and Joseph to be responsible to protect and teach the Christ child?
2. Why did God not give, along with the miraculous birth of Jesus, clear guidelines and understanding on how they should raise him?

3. How do you think Jesus chose when to give in to his mother's wishes, as at the wedding, and when to reject her wishes, as he would do later?

4. Why do our parents' expectations mean so much, even if they never expressed them and even when we are mature and successful?

5. While this tension between mother and child is not something we mature beyond, in what ways can we mature in responding to the tension?

# 4

## The Problem of Authority

### *Deciding How to Respond*

We may say that God wrote his own autobiography. . . . It is unique, because the author appears, personally and without disguise, as a character in his own story; but it is still a story that he is writing, and he is obliged to handle his own character as a character throughout the succession of events. . . . The whole story is contained within the mind of the maker, but the mind of the maker is also imprisoned within the story and cannot escape from it.

Dorothy L. Sayers[1]

A former student of mine, who struggled with much insecurity, once told of a vivid memory from her baby crib. She said that she remembers looking up at her mother from the crib and suddenly realizing that this woman did not know what she is doing. She never hinted that this lovely, respectable, Christian mother was abusive to her then or as she grew up. She merely said that something in her infant mind told her that she was depending on someone who was learning on the job. My student's infant insight is a dramatic and vivid example of a realization that dawns on each of us as we mature. We are dependent on those who give and sustain our lives and livelihoods, whether or not we believe they have our best interests in mind, or if they do, whether or not they are competent to serve our best interests. We gradually realize that those who appear to our childish eyes to be loving caretakers, who are in complete control, are really just human beings like us. Our parents and babysitters and teachers are not in control of their own lives, much less ours.

## Authority Questioning Authority

We grow to understand this reality of needing and questioning authority as we hear our parents talk at the dinner table. Dad and Mom make occasional comments about their parents trying to control their lives and telling them what to do. We learn as we are excused from the table that Dad's father never could hold a job, and the family suffered for it. And Mom, who cannot stand her mother's constant advice about parenting, recalls never finding her mother home after school; she had to work to keep the household afloat.

Likewise, we learn from Sunday lunches that the pastor was a so-so preacher and failed to visit church members when they most needed him. He was not the only one in the church about whom Mom and Dad, not to mention friends who occasionally joined us for lunch after church, shared "concerns." The music minister, the youth leader, and a number of the deacons were less than competent and left much to be desired. We seldom heard the details because we were usually excused to go play so that the adults could talk more freely. In short, those in highest authority over children are the very ones who, by their actions and words, teach them to distrust authority.

## Obedience: The Gift of Authority

Human beings are created to live under, to exercise, and to question authority. Jesus lived not only under the authority of the Father, but he honored and submitted to human authorities as well, even when they were incompetent and corrupt. To be human we have no choice but to live under authority; we were created to do so from the beginning, we are called to do so in the meantime, and we will joyfully and freely do so at the end of time. But for now, for the meantime, what does it mean for our humanity that Jesus in his humanity lived under and exercised authority?

Human beings are to live under authority because we did not author our lives. God is the author of life, the source of our existence. This frees us from the illusion that we are self-made or merely the product of our family, tribe, or culture. God is the author, the originator of all life, and Christ, we are told, is the author and the finisher of our faith, its source and its goal. So authority has to do with authorship—ultimate authority resides in the ultimate author. We participate in the shaping of our own stories, but

53

we did not create their beginnings and we do not control their endings. As Dorothy Sayers points out, the author of all our stories entered into his own creation and submitted to the authority of which he is the source.

Jesus understood that God authorized families, governments, prophets, and apostles to represent his authority in various domains of life. Through his parents he obeyed the authority that would cause him to be born in Bethlehem because of a census decree, to spend his early years in Egypt because of Herod's corrupt use of power, to submit to parents who could not fully understand the mystery of his messianic calling, and to be baptized by the prophet John, who was not worthy to unlace his sandals. He taught from the authority of Scripture as one who had authority. He warned those he taught and healed to submit to the law and to its often-corrupt caretakers at the temple. Indeed, he was clear that he did not come to abolish the law but to fulfill it (Matt. 5:17).

Yet Jesus exercised his own authority as a teacher, often contradicting and indicting Jewish authorities. He performed miracles that defied natural laws. He showed love and forgiveness to the outcasts, in defiance of cultural norms and social mores. In short, his life reveals an ambivalent relationship with human authority, and it witnesses to a way of honoring authority while not always trusting and obeying those who pervert its source and purpose.

## Ambivalence: The Question of Authority

Jesus obeyed the Father, the source of all authority. Not only does the Father send the Spirit by whom Jesus was conceived in the flesh, but also the Father reveals his will to and protects Mary and Joseph, the protectors of Jesus. The same Father was there at the baptism of Jesus to declare his delight in the Son "in whom I am well pleased." Until the Garden of Gethsemane in the last hours before his crucifixion, Jesus trusted his Father without reservation. In those hours of affliction, when he felt abandoned and betrayed, he negotiated with the Father to reconsider this call to the cross. In the end, however, he submitted to the mock trial, the torture, and the execution, but not without questioning, "My God, my God, why have you forsaken me?"

In his relationship to the ultimate authority, Jesus shows us at least two realities about his character and his obedience to authority. First, he reveals that he is truly a son of Israel, because he embodies the very meaning of the name given God's people: "he wrestles with God." He stands in a long tradition of faithful prophets who are not afraid to question why God is doing or not doing this or that: "Why, O Lord?" (Job 16:6–17; Ps. 10:1; 13:1; 73:1; 74). Second, he reveals the shocking truth that we fulfill our humanity when we question authority, even the authority of God. Such questioning is not opposed to loving and obeying God; to the contrary, the mutual love of God and humanity makes the freedom to question not only possible but also healthy. God is the author of humanity, and when the Son became human he submitted to God's authority, even so far as dying, but he was not afraid nor was God afraid when he questioned that authority.

If Jesus obeyed and questioned the authority of God, he certainly obeyed and questioned those people and powers that God authorized. As we discussed in an earlier chapter, Jesus questioned his parents when he was twelve, but he submitted to them and grew in the process. We also have every reason to believe, from what we read about his public life from the age of thirty, that Jesus obeyed the religious and civil authorities. He seemed to have a good reputation in Nazareth, until he went off the deep end and started preaching the Good News of his kingdom. Nor did he teach his followers to defy religious and civil authorities. He instructed those whom he healed to show themselves to the temple priests. He honored Roman soldiers who were under authority and wielded authority. And he honored the paying of taxes, whether to the temple or to Rome.

But he never failed to question such authorities either, just as he had questioned Mary and Joseph. He did so when Jews disobeyed the law of Moses, giving to God the money that should have been used to take care of their parents and divorcing their wives over matters not proscribed in the law. Nor was Jesus kind to those who abused their power of the purse, whether they were Roman tax collectors or temple moneychangers. But he never questioned authority as such; he questioned authority when it defied God's design and demeaned our God-given humanity.

### Defiance: The Challenge of Authority

The seminal insight that Jesus's relationship to authority reveals is that authority is a gift from God to protect, guide, and bless us. As finite creatures with bodies and minds that are unique and fragile, we need those who watch over us as guardians, mentors, and admirers. The Son of

Man enjoyed parents, extended family, and disciples who served him in these three ways and more. As he needed them, so do we.

I remember when I first learned of my need for someone to protect me. When I was a child, I enjoyed playing with my friends after school, on weekends, and in the summertime. What carefree days we spent building tree houses, playing baseball, and taking walks in open fields and scary woods. We laughed, fought, and speculated about the mysteries of life that lay about and ahead of us. I loved almost everything about those kids and those days, except when they wanted to camp out in the field near our houses. It wasn't just that I found the sound of bullfrogs and crickets unnerving, although I did. The truth is, I did not trust my friends' judgment after dark. One of us inevitably invented some mischief that we could inflict on the neighborhood under the mask of darkness. But how could I say to them that I was scared of the dark and even more scared of their character? I couldn't; my mother said it for me: "I just don't want Danny to be out late, because he loses too much sleep." Then I could say, "Oh, Mom, please let me sleep out," and she could refuse, and I would frown until my friends went away. Then I could go watch TV and fall asleep in my bed near those whose characters I trusted and near whom the darkness merely made me sleepy.

## When and How Jesus Defied Authority

Jesus also teaches us when and how to challenge authority. Four examples come to mind of what we can learn from his standing up to and defying authority. The first is the incident recorded by John about Jesus healing the blind man by mixing spit and dirt and applying this miracle mud to his blinded eyes. When the man obeyed Jesus by washing off the mud in the Pool of Siloam, he could see for the first time in his life. As you recall, his neighbors were so astounded that they brought this walking miracle to the Pharisees, who, when the man told them the story of his healing, could only hear that Jesus had made mud and healed on the Sabbath. They even called his parents to interrogate them to admit that this son of theirs was never blind. And the parents, knowing the power of these Jewish leaders, hemmed and hawed, telling the Pharisees to ask their son. Jesus, hearing all of this, asked the man once blind, "Do you believe in the Son of Man?" to which this restored person replied, "Who is he, sir? Tell me so that I may believe in him" (John 9:36). Jesus, of course, says that he is the Son of Man, and the man believes. But Jesus then turns to the Pharisees who witness this coming to faith and calls them blind precisely because they think they see the truth so clearly. In this and numbers of like encounters with hurting people, Jesus teaches us that he and we should not tolerate those who would prevent or look down on the healing and ministry to hurting people for the sake of respectability.

Jesus was equally defiant of those in authority who told lies by preferring their own traditions to the Word of God. For example, when the Jewish leaders, threatened by the crowd's favorable reception of Jesus's teaching, tried to test him and trick him by asking whether a man can divorce his wife for any reason, Jesus recalled to them God's original design that "a man will leave his father and mother and be united to his wife, and the two will become one flesh" (Matt. 19:5). They responded by invoking Moses's teaching "that a man give his wife a certificate of divorce and send her away" (Matt. 19:7). He rebuked them for their hard hearts that used Mosaic law to play fast and loose with God's original intentions and with the human dignity of marriage and women. In other words, these teachers of the law lied in the name of God. Their lies, moreover, sounded wise and practical, and were beautifully argued. Jesus was clear, in later condemning many of these same leaders as whitewashed tombs, that those in authority to teach the truth are of all men the most dangerous liars, for they not only condemn themselves but take down with them those who act on their false teaching. Such teachers, who wield their power with their tongues in the public square, should be confronted by truth tellers in that same public square.

In the two incidents when Jesus drove the moneychangers from the temple—which we will deal with in more detail in a later chapter on anger—we find that he defied systems and customs of authority that had come to accept and tolerate turning "my Father's house into a market" (John 2:16). The people of that time had come to accept this turning of the temple and the holy festivals into a marketplace where priests and merchants conspired to exploit pious Jews who wanted to make offerings to God as they were taught in Scripture. In the name of more perfect sacrifices and with a veneer of piety, these conspirators were cheating and shortchanging their own people. As with the cheap relics sold outside St. Peter's in Rome and the cheap gifts hawked by certain kinds of TV preachers, we just come to accept this exploitation in the name of God. Jesus would have none of it. His words and actions teach and model for us that there comes a time when such systemic idolatry and theft in the name of God must be openly defied and exposed.

The ultimate example of Jesus defying false authority is in his final confrontation with the Jewish authorities that would try, torture, and execute him. He knew this time would come. He became flesh to come to this time. He had skirted Judah and avoided Jerusalem during most of his ministry, but the time came when he was called to stand in this center of Judaism to act and speak the truth in love and let the powers that be have their way with him. This is what Donald Cowan called "getting on your white horse." He admonished educational leaders to avoid such a heroic stand for as long as they could, because "When we get on our white horse, someone is going to die."[2] There came a time when Jesus could no longer avoid the anger, hate, and violence that had stalked him for three years. He had taught as many people as was humanly possible and had healed untold numbers, but now he would do that one deed that alone could be a gift to all people for all time. And there is a paradox here, because this submission to the Father's will was at the same time, on a human level, a complete defiance of the prevailing Jewish authorities and a complete submission to the prevailing Roman authorities. It should not be a surprise that this greatest act of love—that a man should lay down his life for his friends—would be this mysterious mix of defiance and submission or, if you will, defiance for the sake of a greater submission.

### Never Known a Man Like This

How can Jesus's attitudes and actions toward authorities in the first century inform and transform our attitudes and actions in the twenty-first century? No force has challenged the nature of authority, for good or bad, more powerfully than the feminist movement of the twentieth century. Women were tired of being used and abused not only by their husbands, fathers, brothers, and bosses but also by social and economic systems that treated them, in Dorothy L. Sayers's words, as "The Human-Not-Quite-Human,"[3] the title of a provocative and insightful essay by Sayers. In it, she addresses ways the church has failed to address the "Woman Question." She asks how men would feel if they were treated like women. For example, what if a male professor gave an interview to a reporter who then wrote the following: "Professor Bract, although a distinguished botanist, is not in any way an unmanly man. He has, in fact, a wife and seven children. Tall and burly, the hands with which he handles his delicate specimens are gnarled and powerful as those of a Canadian lumberjack, and when I swilled beer with him in his laboratory, he bawled his conclusions to me in a strong, gruff voice. . . ." You get her point! She then adds: "If, after a few centuries of this kind of treatment, the male was a little self-conscious, a little on the defensive, and a little bewildered about what was required of him, I should not blame him."[4] Sayers concludes by contrasting this patronizing attitude of patriarchal societies with Jesus's way of relating to women:

> Perhaps it is no wonder that women were the first at the cradle and the last at the cross. They had never known a

man like this Man—there never has been such another. A prophet and a teacher who never nagged at them, never flattered, or coaxed, or patronized; who never made arch jokes about them, never treated them as "The women, God help us!" or "The ladies, God bless them!"; who rebuked without querulousness and praised without condescension; who took their questions and arguments seriously; who never mapped out their sphere for them, never urged them to be feminine or jeered at them for being female; who had no axe to grind and no uneasy male dignity to defend; who took them as he found them and was completely unselfconscious.[5]

Sayers calls us to a radical humanism that recognizes what Christ saw in women, indeed what he with the Father and the Spirit had created women to be in the beginning, the very image of God and the complement of man. She stands with the apostle Paul against the dehumanizing authorities of his day, "In Christ, there is neither Jew nor Greek, slave nor free, male nor female" (Gal. 3:28).

The question of authority—submitting to it, discerning its legitimacy, and challenging its abuse—is at the very core of being human as Jesus was human. For he who is the author and the finisher of our faith has authorized us to obey when called, to discriminate when uncertain, and to defy when authority is a mere guise for the abuse of power, especially against our neighbor.

### Questions

1. How would you describe your attitude toward authority?

2. What experiences or relationships have most shaped your attitude toward authority?

3. In light of the life and teachings of Jesus, when should we honor and obey authority?

4. How do we know when to disobey authority, and how should we do so?

5. What does the crucifixion of Jesus teach us about authority?

# 5

## The Failures of Jesus

### Why Falling Short Is Okay Sometimes

I should have remembered from my own experience that
students, too, are afraid: afraid of failing, of not understanding, of being drawn into issues they would rather
avoid, of having their ignorance exposed or their prejudices challenged, of looking foolish in front of their peers.
When my students' fears mix with mine, fear multiplies
geometrically—and education is paralyzed.

Parker Palmer[1]

Why do grown men and women, well into successful careers and raising families, still have anxiety
dreams about school? While each person's dream varies
with his or her individual experiences, many can relate to

two standard plots. The first is when we find ourselves in a school hallway surrounded by students who don't seem to notice that we are wearing our underwear, if that. We wander about anxious to find a hiding place or some clothes, but no one seems to pay attention. The other variation is that we are about to take an exam for a course and realize that we never attended the class. The first dream story seems to be about social expectations and pressures that dominate if not tyrannize most adolescent lives. Our own insecurities about our appearance, our peers' constant obsession with how they look, and the cruel comments we make about one another's clothes, skin, hair, bodies, and faces make walking the halls of most high schools like running a gauntlet. The other dream story is about the institutional dimension of school—teachers and quizzes and exams, red ink on essays, and (the worst of all horrors) standardized tests.

### Failure That Haunts Our Lives

While most of us sense from an early age that we fall short of the expectations of our parents, grandparents, older siblings, or other authority figures, school initiates us into the world of systematic, formal, and relentless expectations, evaluations, and disappointments. If in the midst of a loving family and accepting neighbors, our early years never included the taste of failure, schools soon remind us that we fall short of expectations and officially certify and document our failures. And this sense of falling short can be just as real for the student who keeps getting As as it is for the student who is barely passing a subject.

I do not blame schools for creating this sense of failure that haunts so many of our lives. Certainly prior to any formal education, parents instill in their children the sense that they have been measured and found wanting. We do so by saying they disappoint us, they are lazy, or the neighbor's kids could ride their bikes when they were four. When Daddy admires women who have a certain look—tall and slender— or Mommy praises a cousin who is athletic, a short, chunky child knows that she or he can never live up to such standards. And this does not include the cruel and wounding words of the perfectionist parent, the demanding teacher, or the give-150-percent coach. The cumulative message, intended or unintended, is that we fail to measure up.

**We Will Fail**

We all hate to fail. But all humans will fail, and, I would venture to say, most failure is not sin. This struck me some years ago when I and my fellow worshipers were reading aloud a public confession of sins from our church bulletin. The confession had been written by one of the pastors with the intention of making the liturgy of the church more accessible and user friendly. It went something like, "And Lord, please forgive our sins, our mistakes, and our failures." Even before I had a chance to reflect on the prayer a few hours later, I knew something sounded wrong. I understand confessing my sins—my rebellion against God and his Word and my negligence to love him and my neighbor as myself. I am a sinner, as are we all, and I understand how my pride, anger, envy, and sloth harm and destroy people and relationships. But do mistakes and failures equal sin?

Well, I suppose that failing to obey God or to help the neighbor in trouble is sin. But mistakes are also what I make on math quizzes, and failure can be my inability to parallel park on my driver's test.

The simplest definition of failure is to fall short of expectations. These expectations could be my own or from others, and these expectations often are wonderful. We humans flourish when we are full of hope and live life expectantly, wanting to do good things and have good things happen to us. Unlike other creatures, we believe that we can make better lives for ourselves, that our children can surpass what we have done, and that one generation can build upon the work of past generations. Without such expectations, life is at best boring and at worst hopeless. To be human is to live expectantly; to live expectantly means we will fail. To fail is not necessarily to sin.

### Jesus Failed

Jesus failed many times. He failed to live up to his own expectations and desires, first because he was, as we discussed earlier, a finite and embodied person. For example, the Gospels describe his attempts to preach the Good News of the kingdom of God to his family, his neighbors in Nazareth, and to his fellow Jews in Jerusalem. He wanted them to understand that he was the Messiah promised long ago, a Savior to Israel, and a hope to the Gentiles. This was not an act of ego on his part, but the deep desire to share the truth with those closest to him. He failed! We are told that his family, thinking he had gone off the deep end, came to take him by force, if necessary, back home. Even

67

his beloved mother, who knew his calling by miraculous revelation in her own body, could not comprehend what his calling meant, and apparently Jesus failed to enable her to understand. We are also told that he performed many great miracles throughout Galilee and Judea, but he could not do the same in his hometown because of their unbelief. Rather than understanding Jesus, those with whom he grew up simply explained him away.

What he experienced at the fringes of the Jewish world in Nazareth was even more evident at the heart of the Jewish world in Jerusalem: "O Jerusalem, Jerusalem," lamented Jesus, "you who kill the prophets and stone those sent to you, how often I have longed to gather your children together, as a hen gathers her chicks under her wings, but you were not willing" (Luke 13:34). Jesus is not afraid to confess what he longed to do for the people of Jerusalem, in the most tender of terms, and he was free to admit that he failed to fulfill that longing. Indeed, Jesus could not teach, heal, feed, and befriend all people, no matter how deeply he loved them. And this failure was a source of frustration for him. You can hear this frustration with his limits in his response as a child to Joseph and Mary: "Didn't you know I had to be in my Father's house?" (Luke 2:49), and again eighteen years later at the wedding at Cana: "Dear woman, why do you involve me?" (John 2:4). You can hear it when Mary and her sons wait on the edge of the crowd to take him home, and when the crowd informs him that they are there, he replies, "Whoever does God's will is my brother and sister and mother" (Mark 3:35). You can hear his frustration when Peter begins to walk on water and then stops trusting, and Jesus takes his hand and says,

"You of little faith," and when he says to the sleeping Peter, James, and John in the Garden of Gethsemane, "Could you not keep watch for one hour?" (Mark 14:37). Jesus never gave up his great expectations for his disciples, who by the power of the Holy Spirit would do greater things than he would. But in the meantime, they frustrated his expectations.

## Impossible to Please Everyone

Not only did Jesus, the finite human being, fail to fulfill his own expectations for others, he also discovered that often he could not control the responses of those who did hear his preaching and witness his miracles. We think of the Jewish leaders who were angered by his miracles on the Sabbath or of the rich young ruler who understood all too well Jesus's challenge to his self-righteous faith. I think, however, that his apostles were the most persistent frustration to him, because they walked with him almost daily for three years, heard his teaching time and again, and witnessed his miraculous deeds more than any others. Yet they were discouraged by the fact that the Jewish leaders, whom they were taught to respect, hated and opposed him. Having seen him multiply the fishes and loaves to feed over five thousand, they wondered if he could do it again with four thousand. They vied with each other for his attention now and for privileged positions in his future kingdom. Even with one of his closest disciples, Peter, Jesus failed to enable him to face his own pride and fear that would lead to Peter denying his Lord during the most crucial moments of Jesus's life. When they all fled and hid after his arrest, Jesus understood as few human beings ever understand how completely he had failed to prepare his disciples for this cruel crisis. The truth is that unless God absolutely programs us to do his will or we force each other to fulfill our expectations, we cannot control the way others will respond. Some theologians teach us that love cannot force itself. This being true, to love others is to expect and to accept that they will fail to respond as we would like. Jesus knows this.

## Disappointing Those We Love

Not only did the twelve and many other disciples not respond to Jesus as he had hoped and expected, they also were disappointed in him, because they had expectations of their own about what he should have been. Among the most dramatic examples of this is when John the Baptist, then imprisoned, sent one of his own disciples to Jesus to ask, "Are you the one, or shall we look for another?" (Matt. 11:3). God called John from his mother's womb to be the prophetic voice that would make way for the Messiah. He stood in the long tradition of prophets, and Jesus submitted to his authority in baptism and proclaimed him more than a prophet. John, who preached repentance, conversion, and judgment, was not prepared for the Son of Man, who was not going toe to toe with the high priest and Herod. He was not prepared for a Messiah who, it appeared, could not protect John himself from the tyranny of Herod's prison, and who would not later prevent Herod's henchmen from beheading the prophet.

But John's expectations of Jesus, whatever they were, were not unlike those of Jesus's mother, Mary and Martha, a number of the twelve, the Pharisees, and, of course, Judas Iscariot. Jesus disappointed many people. Some had false expectations of him; others had expectations that he would save his people through judgment not suffering; and still others wanted to be rescued by a conquering king, not redeemed by a suffering servant. He failed to live up to their expectations.

Finally, Jesus failed to change God's mind. We will discuss later the suffering of Jesus on the night he was betrayed, but the least we can say now is that Jesus genuinely pleaded with the Father to let this cup pass from him—he did not want to be crucified and God-forsaken. There is an unfathomable pathos and mystery in this exchange between the only begotten Son in whom the Father was well pleased and the Father who had intervened to express his pleasure at Jesus's birth, at his baptism, and at the appearance of Moses and Elijah on the mountain. Again, Jesus failed.

### Failing Gracefully

How strange it sounds to say Jesus teaches us how to fail, gracefully and without sin. If we are to live flourishing lives, full of hope and expectancy, we must learn to fail, and Jesus teaches how to fail. He does so in a number of ways, but perhaps the most basic is that he did not allow his limits as a finite human being in a world of limitless need to restrain his love and compassion for those he encountered. He knew there was more good work to accomplish in this world than one person could possibly attempt. This reality made him face his limits as a human being, who knew that his only infinite act would be to turn his face to Jerusalem, where he would die for the sins of the world. But in letting go of his unique and redemptive ministry, he inspired, encouraged, and foretold that his disciples would do greater things and carry the Good News to the ends of the earth. When most of us come face to face with our limits, we learn to lower our expectations, curb our hopes, and abandon our dreams. Jesus did not. In the face of sin, sickness, hunger, and rejection, he preached and healed, walked and talked, encouraged and confronted, often to the point of exhaustion. Many times he withdrew to a lonely place to pray and rest. There, in intimate conversation with the Father, he seems to have unburdened himself, accepted his inability to minister to everyone in need, and then taken up his ministry with fresh passion. When he could do no more, he blessed his disciples to magnify and carry on in ways that he, supremely human as he was, could not do alone.

## The Freedom to Accept Failure

We learn from Jesus's humanity what a mentor and friend told me when I was first married and deeply immersed in youth ministry. I was at one of those crossroads in my life, when I was trying to decide whether or not to continue a very busy and growing ministry, one in which I was not much older than the students I led, and was barely a step ahead of them in maturity and knowledge. Do I stay with this exciting group of students where we are witnessing the transformation of lives, or do I go to graduate school to learn more about Scripture, ministry, and myself? My friend Harold asked me to go on a walk one day, which is where most of our more serious conversations took place. He listened to me explain my dilemma, and instead of telling me what choice I should make, he simply said, "Most of the important decisions you must make in your life are not between good and evil or right and wrong but between better and best." He went on to say encouraging words about my being a gifted young man with a passion to use my gifts, but he also told me (not necessarily in these words) I would fail to touch every life that needed touching. The question was where I could best invest my life and learn to fail gracefully.

James Fowler thinks that the key to accepting our limits is to know God's calling on our lives—our "vocation." In knowing how God has gifted us and where he has called us to use those gifts, Fowler suggests we are "freed to seek a responsible balance in the investment of our time and energy," which "is the opposite of workaholism." We are also "freed from the sense of having to be all things to all people"[2] because God has also gifted and called others to do his good work in the world. This sense of freedom is evident in Jesus's life when he tells the disciples before he faces the cross that they will receive the Holy Spirit and be witnesses for him, and they will do greater things than he did. They will succeed where he failed. I would add that generations of faithful Christians would succeed where the disciples failed.

### Not-So-Great Expectations

Another important reality that Jesus helps us face is that we will fail to live up to the expectations of others. From the time we can barely walk and talk through our childhood and adolescence, not only are we told the lie by advertisements that we can be anything we want to be, we are also told many subtle messages by people who love us what they expect us to be, or what we suspect they expect us to be. We are bound to disappoint some or most of them. We may choose to be a doctor but not the surgeon they expected. We may go into ministry but not the role or denomination they presumed. It is painful to displease people we would love to please, to fail to live up to their expectations. But the more profoundly we know whom God has made us to become and where God can best use our glorious but limited lives, the more graciously we can say thank you to all those disappointed loved ones.

### God's Expectations

The final lesson in failing that Jesus can teach us is that "we are not our own, we are bought with a price" (1 Cor. 6:19–20). God has given us abundant life and the freedom for which Christ set us free, but God has also placed limits on our lives because of who he is, because of who we are, and because of his larger work as the Creator and Redeemer of all things. At times we will not be able to understand, and we will want to protest, what God is doing. We will fail to comprehend what God is about, and we will fail to persuade God to act differently. Jesus teaches us that questioning God's will is not a sin. There is a way to wrestle with God's will in love, submitting to but not necessarily liking God's will.

Some will tell you that mere failing is sinning, but that is a lie. If we live life with expectancy and do not always live up to those expectations, we will fail. But another and even more insidious lie is this: to fail is to be a failure. Over many years I learned to recognize that this lie was at work in my students. They would come to my desk with a graded essay or test in hand, sometimes with tears in their eyes, and say, "I just don't get it. I don't understand any of this. I am so stupid." In the overwhelming majority of cases I could sit down with them and show them that they did understand most of the material in question. First we would go over all that they did understand; this usually relieved them of the immediate sense of being a complete failure. Then we would go through what they had failed to understand and how they could work on improving.

We can unintentionally instill this sense of being a failure in our children. This occurs when we criticize our children more often and more passionately for what they failed to do than we praise them for what they have succeeded in doing.

## The Freedom to Confess Failure

As the head of a school for many years I enjoyed wonderful opportunities to work with extraordinary teachers and students. I truly enjoyed most of my work. However, two tasks I never learned to like were firing teachers and expelling students. It was always painful. A few times I have been contacted by this teacher or that student to assure me that God used my actions redemptively in their lives. But most of those whom I dismissed I have never heard from since they walked out of my office. I suspect that they still harbor anger and resentment toward me. What helped me through those difficult encounters over many years was learning to say to crying students or angry teachers that, while their behavior or performance merited the action I was taking, I deeply regretted that we failed them. In other words, as a finite human being who fails to do things I want to do, I could not say the fault was all their own. This was important for me to say, because any teacher or employer should expect that everyone in her class or office can do well even though we know that they may fail to meet expectations. When we can live so expectantly, fall short of those expectations so consistently, and still expect the best of others and ourselves, we are free to give ourselves more fully and to fail gracefully.

## Questions

1. Can you recall an incident or relationship in your life when you felt like a complete failure?
2. What is the difference between good, realistic expectations and false, unreal expectations?
3. Have you ever been so desperate to succeed in something that had no God-given moral value that you were willing to sin in order to succeed?
4. In what ways do we frustrate each other with false expectations in our families, friendships, workplaces, and churches?
5. What difference does it make or could it make in our lives if we truly believed that Jesus experienced and understands failure?

# 6

## In Need of Friends

*The Importance of Companions for Life's Journey*

> Friendship is unnecessary, like philosophy, like art,
> like the universe itself (for God did not need to
> create). It has no survival value; rather it is one of
> those things which gives value to survival.
>
> C. S. Lewis[1]

Friendships are risky, but they are a risk we must take. We learn why friendships are risky when we emerge from our circle of family into the larger world, most of us through preschools and play groups. We are thrust into an expanded world, usually without choice, by parents who are ready to get us out of the house. There we encounter a number of kids our age, not our siblings, cousins, and handpicked visitors. We soon learn that these kids, like us, are competing for attention, toys, playground equipment, and companions. Some of them are shy, threatened by anyone who looks at them, and some of them are aggressive, willing and able to command if not tyrannize the entire group. We must find our place in this matrix of confusion, hopefully with some guidance from our parents and teachers, who may have no clue about what is really going on in the midst of this sometimes ruthless pecking order that can seem so cute to those who are long past childish insecurities. Then we find a friend: someone we like, who is like us, who likes what we like, who likes us. All is well, until the next day or the next week when our friend is playing with someone else, and they do not want us to join in. Such, for many of us, is the first experience with risking friendship and finding rejection.

This initiation into the wonders and risks of friendship will play itself out time and again on elementary school playgrounds, in high school cafeterias, in church and community youth groups and summer camps, right into college sororities and fraternities and even in the adult world of the office.

According to Robert Coles in his book *The Privileged Ones*,[2] sons and daughters of the powerful are taught how to pretend to be friends with their teachers and other influential authorities, until they have served their purposes to help advance their ambitions. And if we move into positions of leadership, whether as head of a department in a company, principal of a school, or pastor of a church, we are more often than not mentored by experienced predecessors not to befriend our employees, students, or church members. We are also taught that it is lonely at the top, but why shouldn't it be, when we have chosen to make it lonely?

## The Meaning of Friendship

C. S. Lewis said, "To the Ancients, Friendship seemed the happiest and most fully human of all loves; the crown of life and the school of virtue." He goes on to say, "The modern world, in comparison, ignores it."[3] He does not mean, of course, that modern people have no friends; he asserts that we see no necessity for friendship, much less do we see it as "the crown of life." Lewis goes on to explain that our modern diminishment of the importance of friendship is partly because it is "the least natural of the loves; the least instinctive, biological, gregarious and necessary."[4] In other words, our natural affections for family and our sexual attraction for the beloved are givens in our bodies, our families, and the communities that they make up. But friendship is not such a given. Our choice of friends often begins to set us apart from our parents, our siblings, our spouses, and our biological community. Our choice of friends, unlike familial or sexual relations, does not find its source in our biology but in the recreational, intellectual, artistic, and leisurely choices we make. Lewis says of Eros, "Lovers are always talking to one another about their love" and "are normally face to face." By contrast, "Friends hardly ever [talk] about their friendship. . . . Friends [are] side by side, absorbed in some common interest."[5]

Because life engages our interests in certain ways, we tend to discover that others see the world as we do and find ourselves gazing at the same things in much the same way and finding pleasure in one another's company. In other words, when we say, "I like her," we most often mean "I *am* like her." Lewis does say many marriages start as friendships and end up involving Eros, and many that start in Eros evolve into wonderful friendships. We also can discover as we mature that a parent or sibling or cousin can become a wonderful friend; but they can be a wonderful parent or sibling and never be our friend.

### The Meaning of Jesus's Friendships

Jesus was not a person who found his walk with God the Father, or his own inner life, sufficient to himself. He had a journey to make, as do we all, from birth to death, from baptism to resurrection, and he chose disciples as friends for the journey. His choice of companions included fishermen from Galilee and tax collectors, not to mention prostitutes and other outcasts. He chose among those who chose to follow him. This included the twelve apostles but was far more extensive than this little group. He seemed to enjoy their companionship and confiding in them privileged explanations that they sought after the crowds who came to hear him had gone home. A careful reading of the Gospels reveals that he often confided in scores of such disciples, including telling them of his frustrations and irritations, as companions often do.

But companions, co-workers, and colleagues are not necessarily friends with whom we share our deepest interests and reveal the whole of ourselves. So Jesus did choose from among the scores of disciples twelve with whom he would cultivate a deeper relationship, along with a smaller cohort that included Mary and Martha, Lazarus, Mary Magdalene, Joanna, Suzanna, and others. We rightly believe that Jesus chose them in order to prepare them to take leadership after his death and resurrection. In doing so, he shared with them experiences and teachings on the journey to which others were not privileged. The disciples gave in to the temptations of such privilege, jockeying for position among themselves and attempting to exclude others (children and "those who are not of us," for example) from having access to Jesus. Jesus modeled openness by receiving the children and the outcasts over their protests and by teaching them that the first will be last and the last first. But he did not let this sinful inclination toward pride and exclusivity rob him of the joy of their companionship. Even when he retreated to be alone with the Father, he always knew they would be there to receive him back into their camaraderie.

In the end, on the night he was betrayed, Jesus finally declared openly to them, "You are my friends if you do what I command" (John 15:14). Just before this he commanded them to "Love each other as I have loved you" (15:12). He went on to say that he could call them his friends "because everything I have learned from the Father I have made known to you" (15:15). They were the chosen ones who not only would receive his grace and forgiveness but would share in proclaiming side by side with him the Good News of his kingdom. This was a real friendship. While all of them, except Judas, followed him to the garden so that he could pray before his ordeal began, he chose from among those Peter, James, and John to accompany him to his place of prayer. When he was pleading with

God, which we will discuss in a later chapter, the three of them slept. After he scolded them to watch and pray (Luke 22:46) so that they would not fall into temptation, he returned to his prayers and found them asleep a second time, at which time he said nothing more. Friends accept disappointments from friends.

Friends, unlike parents, children, and siblings, are chosen, not given. Jesus chose his disciples, and they, with some notable exceptions, chose him back. They were there for him with the exception of some who denied him and doubted him, before and after his resurrection. But he stuck by them, and they, for the most part, truly became his friends. He gave his life for them—"Greater love has no one than this, that he lay down his life for his friends" (John 15:13). While this speaks first of Jesus, most of his friends would lay down their lives for the sake of the gospel.

### Risking and Enjoying Friends

Friendships are a fulfillment of our humanity. They are not necessary to be born, to be loved by our family, to marry, or to give life and love to our children. We can do all of these without risking friendships. But we cannot fully know who we are and what we can become if we do not choose to make friends. For friends serve to help us understand our perspectives, our likes and dislikes, our gifts and inclinations. They enable us to discover, express, and celebrate our loves, and to face, articulate, and grieve our deepest hurts. For example, I don't know that Jesus ever regarded his mother as his friend, but we do know that he was able to ask his friend John to take Mary as his own mother. Taking care of Mary was not the point of the friendship between Jesus and John, but friends do such things for one another, because they share a common life, and that which affects one affects the other.

We need friends to discover and express who we are and who we are choosing to become. We also need friends because we live in little worlds. We are all provincial, whether we live on a farm in the Midwest, a small town in the South, or in a world capital. We can know only so many people, enjoy only so many conversations over coffee, and come to know the world through the eyes of only so many friends. Ideally, these limits when expressed in loving friendships do not exclude others or cut us off from the larger world; through them we can embrace others and open ourselves to the larger world. In Jesus, moreover, this is not simply an ideal of friendship, because we are called friends by the one who seeks to call every person a friend. His inclusive love for the whole world prevents Christians who take Jesus seriously from creating the old boys' club and the old girls' circle, where meaning is found in exclusivity.

### Just Jesus and Me?

I want to address one more issue that many of us, consciously or unconsciously, have with needing friends. There have always been among Christians those ascetic, mystical, and pious teachings that would suggest that if we really walked with God, we would not need people. Somehow, needing others, especially friends, seems less than fully spiritual and diminishes the all-sufficiency of God. I would like to answer this concern in two ways. First, from the beginning, God made it clear that we are not only to "glorify God and enjoy him forever" (the Westminster Shorter Catechism) but also to love one another. Before sin entered the world, when sinless Adam walked the earth in perfect relationship with the Creator, God said, "It is not good for the man to be alone" (Gen. 2:18). The two great commandments to love God and our neighbor, quoted by Jesus, are found in the law of Moses. Secondly, when Jesus came to fulfill the law, one of the ways he did so was to choose friends to whom he was as generous in giving himself as the Father had been in giving to him. When Jesus entered into friendships, he transformed them into something larger and more inclusive than they had ever been. Indeed, this small band of Jesus's friends became the most inclusive circle of friends in world history, now numbering, we are told, some two billion.

## Questions

1. In your life, what have been the marks of real friendship?
2. Who are the closest friends of Jesus and what characterized those friendships?
3. In what ways does a lack of friendships diminish our lives?
4. How has your life been enhanced by friends?
5. What does it mean to you that Jesus calls his disciples—then and now—his friends?

# 7

## The Dysfunctions of Jesus's Family

### Learning When to Embrace and When to Resist Our Own Families

All happy families resemble one another; but each
unhappy family is unhappy in its own way.

Leo Tolstoy[1]

A friend of mine told me about a conversation she had
with her sister. As I recall, they were discussing the
differences in their tastes and choice of activities. In the
midst of this sharing of insights into each other's lives, my
friend's sister suddenly observed, "You know, if you weren't
my sister, I probably would have nothing in common that
would cause me to want to know you." Though the sister's
words were blunt and perhaps a bit hurtful, they illustrate

the reality that being born into the same family does not, in and of itself, make us like our siblings.

### Family Values: Refuge or Prison?

Families are wonderful and strange, a refuge and a prison. We often lose sight of this paradox that families embody, especially in the recent debates about "family values." The cause of the debate on the "progressive" side has been the postmodern illusion that we can redefine the family according to our desires. Beginning with the sexual revolution of the sixties, we have experimented with the traditional family for nearly half a century, including an epidemic of divorce, latch-key kids, single parents, blended families, communal families, same-sex unions and marriages, and countless other mutations made possible partly by technological manipulation of the body and society. The wreckage is obvious. Countering this has been the conservative family values movement, which holds fast to the "traditional nuclear family unit" and the happiness and stability it fosters. While holding to a much more historical and religious understanding of the family, this movement also indulges in illusions about both the historical and religious roots of traditional families. Historically, it seems to hold up a model of a 1950s family unit, propagated and preserved in such TV shows as *Leave It to Beaver*. This model forgets that prior to World War II, even in the United States most families were extended families, often housing grandparents, uncles and aunts, and cousins under one roof—a much different family unit. It forgets that women, central to the work and economy of the traditional agricultural

86

family, were stripped of that crucial role by industrialism, later being forced into factories and sweat shops of the late nineteenth and early twentieth centuries. Or they were expected to be the stay-at-home angel who would make a lovely home for her husband and children, "a haven in a heartless world."[2] In short, technologies that have allowed many traditional families to prosper over the past two hundred years have also torn such families apart, while technologies such as birth control, clinical abortion, and countless drug therapies have permitted recent generations to rebel against and reconceive the traditional family.

### Very Good and Very Frustrating

The biblical view that Jesus understood and followed has both a higher and a lower view of family. The higher is that God created the family, beginning with the creation of Eve for Adam, and called this consummation of the creation "very good." Together they would embody the image of God, cultivate the earth, steward creation, and multiply through procreation. In other words, they were created and called to be caretakers, not owners, of God's good gifts: the land, the sea, the air, and the creatures that inhabited them, including their own children. The lower view is that after sin entered the world through Adam and Eve, who rebelled by choosing "to know as God knows," the family became less than this ideal. Indeed, the Scriptures are clear that this divine gift of a man and a woman loving children into being and eventually into their rightful places in the world can become a hellacious tyranny of man over woman, parents over children, and siblings against each other. While never letting go of traditional marriage as a source of love and life, the biblical narratives depict the unvarnished realities of Cain and Abel; Abraham, Sarah, and Hagar; Joseph and his brothers; Moses, Aaron, and Miriam; Saul and Jonathan; David, Absalom, Bathsheba, and Solomon; and I could go on. All of these families in the Bible were dysfunctional, to say the least. Families at their God-given best are indeed sources of life and love, nurturing and launching, refuge and comfort. At their worst, however, families enable some of the most heinous expressions of selfishness and cruelty.

### The Holy Family

When God became flesh, as we discussed earlier, he did so not by a miraculous birth but through an ordinary birth into a traditional first-century Jewish family. We noted that other than the birth stories we find in Matthew and Luke and the glimpse of Jesus when he was twelve years old recorded by Luke, we know nothing about his childhood. But these glimpses do give us insight into his humanity as a baby, a child, and a son of Mary. Likewise, the Gospels give us only glimpses into Jesus's relationship with his larger family, but those glimpses reveal much about how he learned to relate to them. Indeed, Jesus shows us how to love and honor our families for what they have given us while learning to confront and leave them for what they cannot give us.

We spoke earlier of Mary's relationship with Jesus from the time she held him in her arms at the manger to the time she held his dead body in her arms at the cross.

The relationship of mother to child, of child to mother, is unique, and this mother/child relationship surpassingly so. However, sometime after the birth of Jesus, the family of Joseph and Mary became, as do most families, larger and more complicated. The Scriptures are clear that Jesus had siblings, although some Christian traditions would say that they were either Joseph's children by a previous marriage—stepbrothers and sisters—or they were cousins. For the sake of our discussion, it really does not matter. Whether the siblings mentioned in the New Testament were half-sisters and brothers, stepsisters and brothers, or cousins, in the traditions of Jesus's time, they would have been seen as family. It is likely that Joseph died before Jesus was thirty, when he began his public ministry. So when the Gospels describe Jesus's family, they are probably referring to Mary and the other grown children.

Let's reflect on the first of these passages about his family recorded by Mark (Mark 3:21–35). Jesus has just begun his public ministry: teaching, healing, and casting out demons. Vast crowds are following him from all over Israel, even though he is in Galilee avoiding Jerusalem and central Judea, where he knows he will face fierce opposition from Jewish leaders. Just before the encounter with his family that Mark describes, Jesus has chosen the twelve from among his scores of disciples. He then "entered a house, and again a crowd gathered, so that he and his disciples were not even able to eat." So with the fame and the following comes the stress of needy crowds and crowded schedules. Such sudden prominence and pressure apparently worried his family, who heard about it back in Nazareth, some thirty miles away: "When his family

# FLESH-AND-BLOOD JESUS

heard about this, they went to take charge of him, for they said, 'He is out of his mind.'" If these sound like strong words, they are. The term "to take charge of him" is used in other places for arresting or taking a person by force, and the expression "out of his mind" means on the verge of a breakdown or mentally ill. It is especially interesting that Mark, before he picks up on the family again, first tells of the teachers of the law who came from Jerusalem and accused Jesus of "driving out demons by the Prince of Demons." What may we infer from the fact that their accusation that Jesus was demon possessed is bracketed by his family's accusation that he is out of his mind and that they want to take charge of him? It appears that this puts his family in a similar relationship as his accusers. He rebukes the teachers of the law by warning them not to attribute the work of the Holy Spirit to demons, for they risk damning themselves. He more gently corrects his mother and brothers when they want to get to him and responds, "Here are my mother and brothers! Whoever does God's will is my mother and sister and brother."

## The Unholy Family

In responding to their urgent concern in this way, Jesus does at least two things. First, he resists his family's unhealthy and unholy desire to control his life and to direct him away from God's calling on him. As Eugene Peterson translates this passage, "Obedience is thicker than blood" (Mark 3:35 Message). Jesus, who honors his mother and family for what they have done, will not let them control the life that God has willed for him. Such control, he

90

understands, leads to the death of that calling and represents on his family's part an ownership of his life and reputation that does not belong to them.

Their attempt to take Jesus home recalls that possessiveness in parents and siblings I have known who encourage their married children to move back to their hometown, even into the parents' house, forcing the spouse to either follow or divorce. On a more positive note, Jesus not only resists his family's attempt to take charge of his life, he enlarges the vision of what family can mean. All of those who would follow the will of the Father are his mother and sisters and brothers. That is to say, whatever goodness, beauty, and love truly exist in our relationships with parents and siblings prepare us to embrace the larger community, indeed potentially all humanity, as family. Jesus does not reject his family "of origin." He simply acknowledges that family comes from the Father and is intended to open its children to the will of the Father and to the bonds of love among all those who love the Father and whom the Father loves. In other words, Jesus suggests that the intention of family from the beginning was to be a foretaste of what God intends for all humanity.

### Dysfunctional Families, Biblically Speaking

When we consider what we have done to marriages and families, it is amazing that Scripture still maintains them as images of God's relationship with his people. For example, consider the fact that most families mentioned in the Old Testament are dysfunctional, to say the least: Cain kills Abel, Noah commits incest, Abraham fathers Ishmael by

Hagar, Rebekah deceives Isaac, not to mention the polygamy, adultery, rape, and fratricide in the households of Kings David and Solomon. These are the realities of families in a fallen world that the Hebrew Scriptures do not gloss over or explain away. And yet, God calls Israel his bride and speaks of himself as the bridegroom: "For your maker is your husband, the Lord of hosts is his name" (54:5), declares Isaiah in the midst of Israel's unfaithfulness. And that same passion of God for his bride resonates in Hosea's prophecy, when the bride of Yahweh has played the harlot with the idols of the Gentiles.

God reminds Israel through Hosea, "When Israel was a child, I loved him, and out of Egypt I called my son" (11:1). Such allusions to Israel and later Judah as God's children and his bride ring throughout the Prophets. God does not give up on the ideal of family he created in the beginning, as evidenced when he calls Ezra and Nehemiah to expect of his people faithful monogamy with Jewish wives. In short, despite the brokenness of families resulting from their disobedience to God, the biblical ideal and image of the family stubbornly persists right to the time that Jesus walked the earth.

Jesus, holding to this original image of the family, is even more amazing when we consider the other glimpse in the Gospels of his family. We find this described by John (7:1–10), when his brothers suggest to Jesus, "You ought to leave here and go to Judea, so that your disciples may see the miracles you do." Their reason for encouraging him to go on the occasion of the Feast of the Tabernacles, when Jerusalem would be teeming with pilgrims, was because, "No one who wants to become a public figure acts in secret." They conclude very reasonably, "Since you are doing these things, show yourself to the world." We could reason that this is simply fraternal pride and a desire to see their brother embraced by the leaders and people of Jerusalem. But John introduces this encounter by telling us, "Jesus went around in Galilee, purposely staying away from Judea because the Jews there were waiting to take his life." Then John concludes the narration of his brothers' attempt to persuade him to go to Jerusalem by observing, "For even his own brothers did not believe in him." They were setting Jesus up either to be killed or humiliated and rejected. For this was not only the elder brother, certainly a preferred rank in traditional Jewish families, but Mama's boy, whom she treated as somehow more important than the rest of them. Like Joseph's brothers, Jesus's brothers were jealous and angry. They had descended from at least a pretense of "taking charge of him" to protect him—and their family's reputation—from his madness to setting him up for failure, or something worse. But when his family comes to take him away by force, he does not denounce the ideal of family but enlarges it: "Whoever does God's will is my brother and sister and mother" (Mark 3:35).

### Family: Heaven or Hell?

Tragically, this incident between Jesus and his family shows us what family and siblings can become. In *The Great Divorce*, C. S. Lewis tells the story of a dream about a bus ride from hell to heaven. Among those on the bus is a mother who realizes that heaven is full of redeemed folks whom she thought unrespectable on earth if not downright despicable. Rather than accepting the invitation to remain in heaven with her son, her preference is to take him to hell with her.[3] Sadly, what Lewis portrays in fiction is all too real in history and everyday life. From Joseph's brothers who attempted to do away with him to Herod and Caesars who murdered their own children to the headlines of our own newspapers today, the family that was created to be a source of love and freedom can be perverted into a source of suffering, sin, and death. Some who prefer hell to heaven intend to take their families there with them.

Knowing this, Jesus firmly but politely gave his brothers his regrets, and encouraged them to go to the Feast, for his time to face the hate of his enemies had not yet come. They left for the Feast and Jesus, having resisted their attempt to manipulate him, went up to the Feast of Tabernacles in secret, only revealing his presence when he saw fit to do so. His response offers two insights into his relationship with his brothers. First, he discerned their jealous and contemptuous relationship with him and would not give himself to their anger and fraud. On the other hand, he recognized that he could not avoid going to Jerusalem simply because they had tried to manipulate him into doing so for their evil purposes. Not going would have been another way for them to dictate his actions. He may have thought they were right about his public ministry, but for the wrong reason and with the darkest motives.

We need to note here, before discussing what we can learn from Jesus's relationship to his family, that Mark names his siblings (6:3) as Joseph, Judas, Simon, and James. James, who led the Jerusalem church in Acts 15 and penned the New Testament letter of that name, was one of those brothers who we are told once did not believe in him. Families can and do change for the better.

## Jesus's Family Values

We can learn a number of insights about how to relate to family from the way Jesus did. The first is that we should be concerned less about family values—which are mixed at best—than about the truth that God created. When we read what the Bible and the *New York Times* tell us about what families are capable of doing to each other, we would think that God would have dropped both marriage and family as an image and ideal of redemption. But he does not. That which has the potential for the greatest good can also be a source of the darkest evil. So Jesus honored his mother right to the moments before his death, and he did not speak to his brothers with the scathing rhetoric he reserved for the Jewish leaders, even though his brothers deserved it. He knew himself and his calling well enough not to be pressured or controlled by their desire to save him from himself or to expose him to others. He submitted, especially to Mary and Joseph, when God called him to do so. He had to discern the difference between his family's desire that he fulfill God's will and his family's coercive and deceptive desire to preserve their reputations and the status quo.

## The Redeemed Family

The importance of family and how to value them was a crucial lesson I learned from my own father. Will Ray

Russ was a bastard child, born in the coal mining district of Western Kentucky to a mother who, like the woman at the well, was married multiple times in addition to having affairs, such as the one in which my father was conceived. When his mother asked the court to force the man who fathered my dad to help in his support, his biological father said, "You can feed him to the hogs for all I care." He grew up in abject poverty, stealing food from his classmates until he dropped out of school after the fourth grade. Other children beat him up regularly because he was an illegitimate child. An older stepbrother regularly abused him, and he lived in a community so violent that the deacons of the local Baptist church would bring shotguns to church to protect folks from being bushwhacked by the Klan or members of the United Coal Miners Union. He was a boy destined for trouble and destruction, until in his late teens Christ got hold of his life. For the first time he had a Father and brothers and sisters. He took care of his mother, who later became a Christian as well, and tried to treat his half brothers and sisters with dignity and respect. He was by no means a perfect parent to us; many of his flaws, I would later realize, came from such a broken family. But he learned to navigate the memories and realities of that family through his walk with the Savior, who had faced his own broken family with loving discernment.

From Jesus we learn that we can live with dignity and love in the midst of the best and worst of families, not because of a vague or sentimental sense of family values but because God created and Jesus valued family. The family was created out of the imagination of a triune God as an analogy to the relationship shared by the Father, Son, and Holy Spirit. Human families at their best participate in such love. God uses the church, the family of God, our brothers and sisters in Christ, to remind us that human families are a God-given reality pointing to something larger than them.

## Questions

1. What do you value in your family experience?
2. What do you wish you could change about your family?
3. Given how Jesus's brothers treated him, why do you suppose that he tried to honor them?
4. What can we learn from his relationship with his family about speaking the truth in love to our families?
5. What would you have to change in your life to be a redemptive member of your family?

# 8

## Jesus and Sex

### *Daring to See Jesus as a Sexual Being*

Place me like a seal over your heart,
    like a seal on your arm;
for love is as strong as death,
    its jealousy unyielding as the grave.
It burns like blazing fire,
    like a mighty flame.

Song of Songs 8:6

If Jesus "was tempted in every way as we are, and yet without sin" (Heb. 4:15), what were his sexual temptations like? For that matter, what does sexuality look and feel like without sin? How did Jesus embody, understand, and teach about sexuality? While these questions have been variously raised, ignored, and repressed since the early church, they have been raised anew in our times by such popular works as *The Last Temptation of Christ, Jesus Christ, Superstar,* and more recently *The DaVinci Code,* just to name a few. Central to the questions these films raise about the humanity of Christ is "How can Jesus be fully human and not fully sexual?" This raises the important distinction between living day to day as a sexual being and being sexually active—the two are not the same. Could Jesus have been a fully sexual being without being sexually active? It seems unthinkable for our culture, as difficult to understand as men and women who take vows of celibacy as part of their devotion to God, as peculiar as the single people who choose to be single and celibate for all of their life because they feel called to do so by God. But this does seem to be the most reasonable explanation of what we read of Jesus in the Gospels. The response, for the most part, is to assert his sexual purity and deity but not wrestle with the tension Jesus lived with as a fully human and therefore fully sexual person. The real question is, what does it look like to be a fully sexual person, and what does Jesus's actual life as recorded in the Gospels— not concepts or doctrines about his life—teach us about living and embracing the tensions of our own sexuality?

## Unabashed and Unashamed

Before discussing specific incidents and teachings in the life of Jesus, we must first remember that he was Jewish. We tend to gloss over his Jewishness, preferring a more acculturated and pious Jesus, who is after our cultural image and likeness. But the Savior of the world and the head of the church came as a Jewish male who grew up eating and breathing the law of Moses, the Prophets, and the Psalms. We know from our earliest peek into his childhood at the temple "sitting among the teachers, listening to them, and asking them questions" to his passionate cry from the cross, "My God, my God . . ." that Scripture for Jesus was the Hebrew Bible, not the later New Testament. So when asked by the teachers of the law about divorce, he recalled to them the creation theology of Genesis: "For this reason a man will leave his father and mother and be united to his wife, and the two will become one flesh" (Matt. 19:5). We will explore his teaching a bit more later, but for now I want to point out that Jesus grounds his thinking about sexuality in the Hebrew teaching that sex is a gift from God, the fullest expression of which is the marriage of a man and a woman.

By contrast, some of the Greek myths, as expressed by Plato and others, would tell us that sex was a curse given to human beings by the gods, keeping human beings forever confused and diverted by running after their other half to fulfill themselves. The gods used sex to diminish humanity and often used the most beautiful human beings to satisfy their own divine passions (see Plato's *Symposium*). But the Hebrew Scriptures and the Jesus who loved and taught them viewed sexuality as a fulfillment not only of our humanity but also of the image of God in humanity. The only two times that Genesis mentions that we are created in the image of God, it echoes, "male and female he created them" (Gen. 1:26–27; 5:1–2). The strong implication here is that Adam or Eve alone did not embody the image of God, but the two together, becoming "one flesh," were the fulfillment of God's image. This profound and unique understanding of human nature is not Platonic or spiritualized, for the passage Jesus quotes about the two becoming one flesh is followed immediately by, "The man and his wife were both naked, and they felt no shame" (Gen. 2:25). My point is that the mind and imagination of Jesus was fully formed by the Hebrew Scriptures, which are unabashed and unashamed about human sexuality.

## Jesus and Testosterone

Not only was Jesus fully Jewish, he was born a male, with all of the implications of what that means. He was circumcised on the eighth day, raised as a boy, was a carpenter's son and apprentice, became a rabbi, and moved in a man's world. These matters of fact from the Gospels have either been glossed over by ascetic and pious theologies over the centuries, or they have been realities and mysteries that have fascinated Christians since Jesus walked the earth. Art historian Leo Steinberg describes and reflects on these realities and mysteries as depicted by scores of Renaissance artists. His book *The Sexuality of Christ in Renaissance Art and in Modern Oblivion* includes scores of images of the baby Jesus with genitals prominently shown and the crucified or resurrected Lord with genitals either shown or barely covered. Many of those paintings about the infant Jesus are of the wise men that came to worship him, and they often are gazing at his genitals, not in some salacious or prurient manner but to confirm his true humanity. Likewise, there are paintings of Mary touching the genitals of her son, of others looking upon

101

them with wonder, and of angels spreading flowers on them. Steinberg explains such paintings: "Their central subject is the marvelous proof offered to the Three Kings: God, come to dwell humanly among men, exposes his frailest member—whether to the knife, the touch, or the steadfast gaze of the faithful—in order to dispel mistrust of his Incarnation forever."[1]

In other words, these paintings were painted by orthodox, often pious Christians who did not see the sexuality of Jesus as diminishing his divinity but as a sign that God has fully entered our humanity, not only redeeming it but also redefining it. The Jesus of the Gospels and the one that these artists painted was a Jewish male who embraced his humanity, including his sexuality, without diminishing and distorting his sexuality into self-centered carnal satisfaction.

### Learning Sex at Home

Jesus learned what it means to be sexual at home, from Mary and Joseph, from his siblings and cousins. I start here because this is where we too learn to be sexual. This was the shocking insight that Sigmund Freud, himself a secular Jew, recovered for the modern world when he wrote his scandalous essays on infant sexuality, making the commonsense observation that we first learn healthy or unhealthy attitudes about the opposite sex and our own sexuality from our mothers and fathers. We may later receive sex education from the locker room, slumber parties, salacious movies, dirty jokes, and pornography. If we are fortunate we will learn about sexuality from affectionate parents, healthy conversations with wholesome adults, honest literature and movies, and gazing on human beauty. But long before the arousal of adolescence, we have witnessed and been taught what it means to be male and female. Or to put a different spin on a modern expression, in the embrace of the family Jesus learned what it means to be truly sexual: not merely to have sex but to have love and children and community within the embrace of a covenant of marriage. As we discussed earlier, Jesus also learned through his relationship with Mary how to love a woman without being possessed by her. This fully Jewish, fully Christian, and fully human understanding of sexuality is quite the opposite of "having sex" or "hooking up" or the even more vulgar and dehumanizing expressions we use to describe two people who are doing anything but intercourse.

So Jesus, this Jewish male schooled in sexuality in the wholesomeness of a loving if not always understanding family, ventured into his ministry at thirty years of age a celibate. While affirming marriage and the "two becoming one flesh" in his rebuke of the teachers of the law and their easy-come-easy-go attitudes toward divorce and women, Jesus chose for the sake of his calling to remain celibate while being fully sexual. Indeed, if Jesus had no sexuality, his celibacy would be nonsense; he would simply be neutered in body and mind. But he was not. Several incidents in his life reveal how honestly and lovingly he embodied his sexuality.

### Living Sexually in the World

Jesus's meeting with the Samaritan woman is among the sexually charged narratives in ancient history, though countless preachers and scholars have managed to ignore the sexual tension just beneath the surface in favor of seeing this encounter as an object lesson for evangelism. When Jesus meets this woman, he meets a person who is his very opposite: Samaritan, female, and promiscuous. At about noon, the disciples are in town buying food, while Jesus rests at Jacob's well. When the woman arrives to retrieve water, Jesus asks her for a drink. She is shocked, and this woman, we discover, is not easily shocked, since she has been married five times and is now living with a man. A Jewish man is speaking to her, and they are alone. Now let's face it, even if the two of them are the most wholesome human beings on earth, this is a sexually charged situation, especially in the ancient world when men and women were segregated from one another in almost all arenas of life other than the home. She responds, whether in surprise or coyness, "You are a Jew and I am a Samaritan woman. How can you ask me for a drink?" I suspect that a woman who has been married five times and is now living with a man sees all men as sexually needy and exploitive. After all, it was common knowledge that Jewish rabbis were not permitted to speak with women in the streets.

It quickly became evident to the woman that this man was not flirting or making salacious remarks about "living water." Indeed, he asked for her husband, and when she responded that she had no husband, he confronted her with her moral condition, especially as it related to men. Immediately, this wily woman of the world turned the conversation to religious distinctions between Jews and Samaritans, but Jesus turned it right back to her need to face up to things as they really were. She was shocked for much deeper reasons than what first startled her; here was a man who was not hitting on her, was not judging her, and was interested in her redemption. She was prompted by the disciples' arrival to break off the conversation and go to town to tell her townsmen, "Come, see a man who told me everything I ever did" (John 4:29). Assuming that these people had known her all her life in this small town, they may have first gone out to hear how Jesus's revelations about this woman matched up to the town gossip. When the disciples returned, they were shocked that Jesus was talking with a woman—alone—not that he was talking with a Samaritan, which was bad enough.

Jesus did not fear, nor was he seduced by, a woman whose "sexiness" was powerful and bold. He took advantage of the opportunity (not the woman) by meeting her fetching and promiscuous persona with honest love that refused to let her demean herself or him but equally refused to stop at judging her for her life of immorality. He saw through her longing for a semblance of love, her thirst for fake affection, and called her to quench her deepest desires. She responded by giving herself to him in the depths of love that make mere sensuality a cheap substitute. In short, this woman was more a woman than she had ever been, because she had encountered a real man. He did not flirt with her or flatter her. Indeed, he confronted her "with everything she had ever done," but he did so that she might live a redeemed life, including a redeemed sexuality.

## Living Sexually in Our Bodies

Jesus not only redeemed the sexuality of others but was at home with his own sexuality, as we see in two separate but similar encounters recorded in the Gospels. The two incidents are, understandably, confused in many of our minds.

I refer first to a woman anointing Jesus with oil and washing his feet with her tears and hair. Only Luke, early in Jesus's ministry, records the incident. While reclining at the table, a woman locally known as a "sinner" "brought an alabaster jar of perfume, and as she stood behind him at his feet weeping, she began to wet his feet with her tears." If this is not embarrassing enough, Luke goes on to say, "Then she wiped them with her hair, kissed them and poured perfume on them" (7:37–38). Astonished at this brazen behavior, the Pharisee host, Simon, accuses Jesus in the most understated way, saying to himself, "If this man were a prophet, he would know who is touching him and what kind of woman she is—that she is a sinner" (Luke 7:39). While you could cut the air with the sexual tension created by this "kind of woman," Simon does not accuse Jesus of being a whoremonger. For the one who is truly shameless here is Jesus. He is neither titillated nor embarrassed by her touch and attention. So Simon focuses not on Jesus the lusty rabbi but on the fact that he could not be a prophet, because a prophet would know "what kind of woman she is" and be ashamed to be seen with her.

In our world, this kind of composure about sexually charged encounters is associated with a man of the world, a James Bond who loves and leaves—or kills—without ever losing his cool. By contrast, preachers and priests are usually depicted as either hypocritical seducers or blushing prudes—but not Jesus! He accepts her touch and her tears as expressions that "she loved much" in the only way such a woman knows how to love—physically. But she who has probably slept with many men knows that loving this man is not about lies and seduction but about truth and forgiveness. Indeed, the only obscene thing that Jesus says in this encounter, at least from the perspective of the guests, is, "Your sins are forgiven," and "Your faith has saved you; go in peace" (Luke 7:48–50). He not only knows she is a sinner, he is brazen enough to assert that he can forgive sins and confer salvation and peace. True God and true man.

### Uniquely Sexual

The second encounter, a separate incident, is recorded by Matthew, Mark, and John (12:1–8) and occurs in the last days of Jesus's life, when Mary, Martha, and Lazarus invite Jesus to dinner, just before he enters Jerusalem to face his arrest and crucifixion. We are told, in John's words, "Then Mary took about a pint of pure nard, an expensive perfume; she poured it on Jesus's feet and wiped his feet with her hair." Now in this version, even in Matthew and Mark, who do not tell us that the woman is Mary of Bethany, there is no mention of her being a "sinner." There is only a tirade, led by Judas, that this perfume could have been sold "for more than a year's wages and the money given to the poor." Jesus replies that this woman, out of love, is preparing his body for his funeral, and her act will be retold "wherever the Gospel is preached throughout the world." What an extraordinary response! A pious woman like Mary imitates, I assume, the earlier loving act of a "sinner." No one even hints at what Simon and his guests had thought and said earlier about the sexual connotations of such an act. Perhaps this is because they know that Mary is a pious disciple of Jesus. Perhaps they have seen Jesus in so many encounters with women, including the woman with the issue of blood and the woman caught in the act of adultery, that they know better than to believe that his manhood depends on sexual chemistry and manipulation. He can be sexual without sexualizing every loving act, every affectionate look, and every female touch.

As in every human dimension of the life of Jesus, we cannot forget that he is also truly God. Indeed, he is the fullness of the image of God in human form. Since he is the God/Man, I presume that his sexuality and sexual desires do not carry in them that same incompleteness that we mere humans, including sinless Adam, experience. "It is not good for the man to be alone" (Gen. 2:18). The creation story in Genesis clearly states that humanity was not fulfilled in the image of God, not "very good," until God made Eve and the two became one flesh. To put it differently, both times that Genesis says that God created humans in his image, it follows with "male and female he created them" (Gen. 1:26–27; 5:1–2). This is the reason that the first symptom of Adam and Eve's sin was the realization that they were naked, and they were ashamed. That is, before they hid from God and experienced their broken relationship with him, they experienced the broken image of God in them, male and female, ashamed and accusing. Jesus, by contrast, never exhibits shame about his body and his sexuality. To the extent that his divine nature enables this, it does so no more or less than in any other dimension of his humanity. Some might say that he could live his sexuality so redemptively because he was also God and that's not fair. As C. S. Lewis reminds us in *Mere Christianity*, such logic is like a drowning man saying the person standing on the shore throwing him a rope has an unfair advantage. Lewis remarks, "That advantage—call it 'unfair' if you like—is the only reason why he can be of any use to me."[2]

### Learning to Live Sexually Like Jesus

So how can Jesus "be of use to me" in living as a sexual being in a fallen world? First, Jesus's life and teaching reveal to us that our sexuality is more than "sex"—having sex, being sexy, sex acts, giving off sexual signals, and so on. In the image of God we are sexual creatures, not just in adult consenting relationships but also in our whole being. We are born male and female. We live our relationships as male and female. We see the world as male and female. We embody our family, community, and culture as male and female. Without denying the fact that different cultures, different historical eras, and even different families live out that sexuality differently, the point is that sexuality pervades every dimension of our lives. We relate to our sons and daughters, our mothers and fathers, our sisters and brothers differently.

While my wife is the only woman with whom I have a lifelong covenant of love and with whom I am sexually intimate, she is not the only woman in my life. Long before I married Kathy, my mother helped form my understanding of being a male, and although she has passed on, she still helps shape my sexuality. Likewise, my father did the same and still does. And my daughters are significant women in my life, and now so is my daughter-in-law. This not only means that my understanding of and relationship to women is larger than my relationship with my wife, it also means that Kathy does not have to carry the burden of being the totality of womanhood for me. Or to put it back in the context of Jesus's life, Mary was not "the virgin Mary" to him; she was mother and also follower and eventually disciple. This view of sexuality, whether we are married or single, means that marriage in general and lovemaking in particular does not have to carry the full weight of our sexuality. They are given a context that acknowledges their deep significance while not reducing sexuality to these two ways of being sexual.

Secondly, from Jesus we learn to face and embrace our sexuality, even though it is so often perverted by our sinfulness. Jesus understood fully the sinfulness of human nature and witnessed the way it destroyed persons and families. However, unlike with many of the ascetic traditions, in his time and our own, he never hints that sexuality is the problem. He honored marriage, whether making wine in Cana or denouncing divorce to the teachers of the law. He spoke parables that depict marriage and marriage feasts in the highest terms. He takes up the Hebrew image of God as the bridegroom and his people the bride. He faced the perversions of sexuality with total honesty, no shame, and deep grace and forgiveness. In short, from him we learn that our struggles with our sexuality need to be faced, confessed, and redeemed, not hidden, denied, and repressed. There is no hint that the answer to sin in sexuality is "get thee to a nunnery," to quote Hamlet. Jesus does not lecture the prostitute or the woman at the well about the evils of the body. He simply acknowledges that they have sinned in their bodies, in their sexuality, and asks them to face up to this, to sin no more, and to go their way as fully sexual beings.

**Heavenly Sex**

In Jesus, sexuality is not merely about this world—carpe diem, eat, drink, and be merry—because he entered, redeemed, and elevated sexuality as eternal. When he walked this earth in a resurrected body there is no hint that he did so as an angel. His disciples, from the tomb to the day of his ascension, recognized him as a man. While he clearly teaches that in heaven there will be no marriage, he does not say there will be no sexuality. What that sexuality will be like, we are not told, any more than we are told what daily life and feasting will be like. Steinberg, the art historian cited earlier in this chapter, suggests, "The resurrected, both male and female, shall not be ashamed in heaven." He goes on, "This is self-evident to St. Thomas Aquinas, who writes, 'Though there be difference of sex there will be no shame in seeing one another, since there will be no lust to invite them to shameful deeds which are the cause of shame.'"[3] Here we have a medieval monk and theologian, himself a celibate, who can imagine that heaven will be fully sexual, without shame and guilt. I will not explore this mystery further, except to suggest that in Jesus

111

we not only learn to embrace our own sexuality and that of our fellow human beings in this life, but we also learn that such redeemed sexuality is part of our humanity in the next life.

## Questions

1. In your life, has Jesus been the understanding older sibling with whom you could talk to about sexual questions and struggles?
2. Why is it so difficult for many of us to imagine Jesus as sexual, or if we do, we imagine him as sexually active?
3. What early impressions did you have about love, marriage, and sexuality from your family?
4. How can we learn from Jesus to accept and be aware of our sexuality without sexualizing all relationships?
5. In what ways does a biblically wholesome attitude toward our sexuality take the pressure off of marriage as the total expression of our sexual natures, whether we are married or single?

# 9

## Good and Angry

### *Passion with Purpose in a World of Violence*

Such an anger alone is criminal which is against
charity to myself or my neighbor; but anger against
sin is a holy zeal, and an effect of love to God and
my brother, for whose interest I am passionate,
like a concerned person; and if I take care that
my anger makes no reflection of scorn or cruelty
upon the offender, or of pride and violence . . .
anger becomes charity and duty.

Jeremy Taylor[1]

learned about anger before I was old enough to know
or pronounce the word. I grew up, like so many others,
in a family and community where anger was the easiest
emotion to express and was, for the most part, acceptable.

Most of the time I experienced it when my mom or dad gave me that look that could burn holes through a person. I occasionally felt the sting of a belt, rarely a switch, but mostly the sting of furious words. Even worse were those times when I witnessed my parents staring and speaking at one another that way. I usually knew why they were angry with me and mostly deserved their ire, but the fury being exchanged between them in those stares and words were a dark mystery to this child's mind. I knew before I was ten years old that my family was a fragile thing and that love and anger were its major passions.

My father owned a small construction firm, which is how he made a decent working-class living for our family. He was also an ordained minister and often preached at revival meetings in a number of churches. He would come home from a long day of pouring concrete or plastering walls, eat, clean up, and head out by himself to preach, leaving my mother to take care of four boys. One evening he came home and seemed agitated. I was still awake as he went to the closet where he kept his guns, loaded a shotgun, and went out to the back steps of our little house and sat down with the shotgun across his lap. I remember—whether I saw it or was told later what happened, I don't really know—a car drove slowly down the alley behind our house, until it had a clear view of the house, my dad, and the shotgun, at which point the driver and his companion slammed on the accelerator and squealed down the street at the end of the alley, never to return. We were told later that my dad's sermon that night had moved two women to ask Jesus into their lives and to denounce their sexual immorality, which the two fellows in the car had been enjoying. They were going to get my father. That was my first experience of how easily anger could spill over into violence.

## Striking Close to Home

I wish I could say that was my last and worst experience with anger, but I learned firsthand fighting my brothers, my neighbors, my classmates, and even strangers how easily anger turns to violence. However, no such experience burns in my memory greater than the anger I unleashed on our oldest child, Libby. She was about four years old at the time and sitting in the front seat of our little Honda Civic, which was not air-conditioned, gabbing away and asking endless questions while Kathy slept and smirked in the backseat with our younger daughter, Marie. We had driven about eight hundred miles that day, returning from a visit with Kathy's family. In order to save money, of which we had little, we drove as long and hard as possible. It was hot and sticky, and the only way to get relief was to roll down the windows at sixty miles per hour and be battered by the hurricane-force winds, or to sip on a cold drink.

It was getting late, so we decided to take a break and try the cold-drink alternative. We put our money in one of those old soft drink machines where a cup drops down, your selected drink pours into it, and ice plops into the cup. We each made our selection and headed back to the car to endure another leg of this hellish trip. I instructed Libby to sit down, buckle up, and hold her drink carefully and to watch out for my drink, which was sitting somehow between us—no cup holders in those days. I slipped behind the wheel, at which time Libby proceeded to bump my drink so that it spilled right into my lap, just as I had warned her not to do. I then did what any mature father would have done: I took what little drink remained in the cup and threw it into my four-year-old daughter's face. She was horrified and burst into tears; I was ashamed and humiliated and burst into hugs and apologies. She was, of course, very accepting of my plea for forgiveness, and Kathy and I swore we would take out a loan for a motel before we would put our family through such a nerve-wracking day again. But I knew from that moment how easily peevish anger, mixed with fatigue and minor frustrations, can become a violent fury, even against those we love more than anyone else on earth.

### The Power of Anger

Anger is a powerful passion that can destroy families, friendships, businesses, churches, and nations. Yet the Gospels show and tell us that Jesus was angry a number of times and for a variety of reasons, just as we are told hundreds of times in the Old Testament that God was angry. Is such a description of God or Jesus simply metaphorical language, as some have suggested, for a passion that is totally unlike human anger? The incidents of anger in the life of Jesus certainly look like what the rest of us experience and witness as anger. If it is not, then Jesus was not tempted in this area of character and temperament that affects and influences so many of our lives in such damaging ways. I think that the Gospel stories clearly describe Jesus as experiencing anger. But the way he experienced it and the ways he embodied it show us that anger can be a

redemptive passion that awakens us to our potent
to life's injustices. In short, we learn through Jesu. . ...
what Paul means when he writes, "In your anger do not
sin" (Eph. 4:26).

Anger is so often destructive, and Jesus did teach, "Anyone who is angry with his brother will be subject to judgment" (Matt. 5:22). Moreover, Paul lists anger among "the works of the flesh" alongside fornication, adultery, idolatry, jealousy, envy, and drunkenness (Gal. 5:19–21). In light of these and other passages that warn that anger is so often sinful, it is easy to understand why there have been those in the history of Christianity who deny that Jesus was truly angry. The heretical version of this denial is best expressed in the early church leader Marcion who "wanted a Christianity free from every vestige of Judaism," in the words of Abraham Heschel.[2] Marcion so detested the angry God of the Old Testament and any hint of him in the New Testament that he proposed a canon of Scripture that would only include Luke, Acts, and select epistles. This heresy was rejected by the church, but a number of prominent church fathers still had problems with the idea that God could be angry. According to Heschel, a number of these early church leaders were heavily influenced by the Greek ideal that the divine being is an unmoved mover, an impassible deity whose character could not participate in the flux of anything like human emotion.

I would also suggest that Christians have been turned off to the reality of an angry God or an angry Jesus because of the various ways preachers have attempted to scare us with visions of fire and brimstone throughout the ages. One can find such teaching in the writings of medieval priests, in Jonathan Edwards's "Sinners in the Hands of an Angry God," in James Joyce's description of young Stephen's Catholic education in *A Portrait of the Artist as a Young Man*, and in the many TV preachers who haunt late-night cable channels.

## Passion with Purpose

But if we are to face the truth in our own lives, as well as in the Old and New Testaments, we cannot deny that anger is a passion that is both divine and human, and, in Jesus, we witness a way of being angry without the sin and violence that anger often engenders. To suggest, as a number of great church leaders have done, that the anger of Jesus was metaphorical is to divorce him from the God of Abraham, Isaac, Jacob, and David. It is to make of him some kind of passionless pretender to our humanity. This is not the Jesus described in the Gospels. He was most passionate, and anger was one of his many passions, but he was always angry with a redemptive purpose.

I see in Jesus's life at least three kinds of good anger. The first and most common source of anger Jesus experienced and expressed was frustration. He was frustrated mostly with his family and friends, those closest to him, those who so often failed to understand him, his calling, and his teaching. Of course, no one frustrates us quite the way our family can. Jesus is no exception. You can hear it in his twelve-year-old voice when he asks Mary and Joseph at the temple, "Why were you searching for me?" You hear it again in his thirty-year-old voice at the wedding when he responds to his mother's volunteering him: "Why do you

118

involve me?" The note of frustration and rebuke are even stronger when Mary and the family think that Jesus has gone mad and have come to take him home. When he is told that his mother and brothers are outside, he retorts, "Who are my mother and brothers?" He then answers his own question: "Whoever does God's will is my brother and sister and mother" (Mark 3:35). Jesus loves Mary and his family. But she of all people should know by revelation from angels who he is, and his siblings grew up with him and must know his character and calling. Jesus should expect more understanding from them, and they deserve to hear the angry edge in his voice. This same sharp tone is also heard by his disciples when they fail to understand his teaching, when they are frightened at his calming the storm ("Where is your faith?"), when they seemingly forget that he can feed thousands with next to nothing, and when they cannot understand that he must suffer and die. This is the quality of daily anger that any one of us can feel for those closest to us, those who know us best, and those for whom we have the highest expectations.

### Redeeming Anger

A second kind of anger that Jesus expressed is what I will call harnessed anger. It arises out of the same sense of high expectations for people you love, but it is the creative anger of the teacher. Jesus was a rabbi, a teacher. Teachers love people by enabling them to learn. To do so, a teacher must arrest his students' attention and focus their very being on the knowledge, skills, and wisdom that will forever transform their minds and imaginations. Likewise, teachers must expect the best of their students. In the years that I taught high school students, I often found that I thought more highly of them than either they or their parents did. Parents would sometimes scold me for the level of literature or writing I expected of their children: "You can't expect ninth graders to read *Oedipus Rex* or Job, much less to write with any understanding about what they have read." I could only reply that I did expect this and, indeed, they did read, understand, and write about it. To capture students' minds and imaginations and to lead them to understanding is hard work motivated by great expectations. Such expectations lead to great disappointments when students just don't get it. This frustrates and angers teachers, and Jesus, the master teacher, was no exception.

But teachers know that the creative energy arising from our students' failures to learn can be a motivating and captivating force. For example, Jesus confronts the hypocrisy and fury of the Pharisees with his own stern anger. Luke tells us (11:37–52) that once they invited Jesus to eat with them, and they were surprised "that Jesus did not first wash before the meal." Jesus, seeing their smug and self-righteous behavior, rebuked them: "Now then, you Pharisees clean the outside of the cup and dish, but inside you are full of greed and wickedness." He then exclaimed, "You foolish people!" This is followed by Jesus proclaiming six specific ways in which they were religious frauds. By the time he finished his tirade against them, they were furious and conspired how to shut him up permanently.

By harnessing his anger at these pious frauds, Jesus does two things. First, he confronts them with their self-righteous sins and does so methodically and graphically. Perhaps by hearing such a shocking diatribe against their culture of pride and deceit, one or more of them might see himself as Jesus sees him: a beloved sinner. But if he does so, he will come like Nicodemus, in the shadows and apart from his pious peers. Secondly, and more importantly, Jesus's angry tirade arrests the attention of his disciples. We cannot forget that the men Jesus denounces are the ones whom his followers were taught to admire. By exposing the Pharisees as frauds, Jesus creates in his followers great fear and confusion about who they are, what they should aspire to become, and, of course, Jesus's role in their lives. Knowing this, after the teachers of the law have left in rage, Jesus turns to the crowd following him and opens one of his most splendid teachings by saying, "Be on your guard against the yeast of the Pharisees, which is hypocrisy!" (Luke 12:1). He then goes on to address their fears about angering such powerful men by reminding them with analogies to sparrows, ravens, and wildflowers that he is the only one to fear and, fearing him, they have nothing to fear. Many of these people would shortly face oppression, persecution, imprisonment, and execution. They needed to hear these and other teachings of Jesus to prepare them for the hard times after Jesus ascended to the Father.

## Righteous and Indignant

I must quickly add that Jesus was not pretending to be angry. He was angry. But he controlled the anger for redemptive purposes. However, there were times when

Jesus expressed what we have come to call righteous indignation, the third kind of anger. The actual word for anger that we translate *indignation* is attributed to Jesus only once, by Mark. Jesus was walking with his disciples and overheard them arguing with each other about who was the greatest in the kingdom of God. So Jesus sat down, called a little child to stand among them, and took the child in his arms, saying, "Whoever welcomes one of these little children in my name welcomes me; and whoever welcomes me does not welcome me but the one who sent me" (Mark 9:37). He went on about how highly God values these little ones. A few minutes later, when people brought little children for Jesus to bless, the disciples rebuked them. When he saw them do this, Jesus "was indignant." He was angry for those children facing the indignity of men rejecting them as if children are worthless. His rebuke of his disciples was full of indignation, because they not only rejected these little ones but also rejected him and his teaching.

The only time that Jesus shows greater fury is when he drives the moneychangers from the temple. Here he actually uses physical force to show his indignation. Indeed, he does so twice: once early in his ministry as told by John and once near his crucifixion, as told by Matthew, Mark, and Luke. Both times it was near the Passover Feast. Tens of thousands of Jewish pilgrims gathered in Jerusalem for this great high feast. Where such crowds gathered, there was money to be made, especially since thousands needed to buy animals for sacrifice at the temple. Prices went up and folks were short-changed. Knowing this, as everyone did, Jesus was furious at these people who profiteered off of God's temple and God's people. John says, "So he made a whip out of cords, and drove all from the temple area, both sheep and cattle; he scattered the coins of the money changers and overturned their tables" (John 2:15). He then turned to these exploiters and said, "Get these out of here! How dare you turn my Father's house into a market!" (John 2:16). His fury stops short of doing violence against any people, but his words and actions speak for themselves. Human beings of power and privilege who exploit the powerless, oppress the needy, bring offense to children, and do so self-righteously in the name of God are performing deeds that are outrageous, and the response should be outrage. Religious and political leaders who bring indignities on those whom they are supposed to serve deserve our indignation. The outrage and indignation of Jesus was fully human and not sin.

### Good and Angry

Some Christians would remind us that we are not Jesus, and I could not agree more. Indeed, left to our fallen humanity, our anger is capable of terrorism, spousal abuse, violence against children, and enough rage to murder strangers who cut us off on the highway and family members who demean us one too many times. I am very conscious of sinful anger, because while I have been writing this chapter I have also been following the story of the mass murder of thirty-two students and faculty members at Virginia Tech, not to mention listening to the daily body counts in Iraq. But we cannot deny in the life of Jesus and in the teachings of the Old and New Testaments that there is also good anger—anger that arises from high expectations for those we love, that gives rise to creative ways of teaching our children and our students, and that expresses outrage when the least among us suffers indignities at the hands of the powerful.

Jesus was good and angry.

## Frustration as Love

Let me suggest at least three insights that come from Jesus's example. First, we must learn to live in the tension of frustrated anger toward those closest to us—family, friends, students, and colleagues—as long as we have high expectations for them and they frustrate those expectations. We must find kind, good-humored, and gracious ways to express such frustration, so that they know that our anger at these petty disappointments is an expression of love. Without these, they don't know if they are loved. We are like a student who lived in the dormitory where Kathy and I served as directors while in graduate school. He shared with us that he always felt insecure and unloved, because his father never expressed any anger when he failed or did something he knew was wrong. The father never raised his voice, much less his hand, against his son. He just acted disappointed. The student then went on to say that he figured that if he was not worth getting angry about, he was just one of his father's disappointments. It made him feel worthless and hopeless. People need to know that we have such high hopes for them that when they fall short of their potential, it frustrates us precisely because we think so highly of them.

### Educating Through Anger

Likewise, from Jesus we can learn to harness anger as creative energy to capture the attention of those we want to teach. Since I am a teacher, I naturally think of examples I have witnessed in other teachers. My mentor and friend, Dr. Louise Cowan, a professor of literature, gave me the most vivid example of the pedagogical power of anger in a graduate class that she taught. This regal and wise professor loved her field and loved her students. She was both stern and kind. I still have a blue book that she returned to me, in which she commented on my careful analysis of a poem: "A sensitive misreading of the text." You get the picture. But she also believed in her bones that study of literature is a privilege and that the classroom is sacred. One day she called on three of us in a row, none of whom were prepared to discuss the reading for the day. She then scanned the entire class and commenced delivering an impassioned speech about the sacredness of the classroom and the sacred privilege of the student and teacher. At the end of this eloquent intellectual thumping, she closed her book, picked up her handbag, and left us sitting there. Needless to say, we were prepared and attentive the rest of the term. Years later I asked Louise about that incident. She laughed and said that she had delivered such a speech only a few times in her career, since one must use such a tactic sparingly. While she was indignant and she meant every word of it, she was in complete control and knew exactly what she was doing.

I have observed this same experience of anger transformed into creative pedagogy in three more of my favorite teachers—my daughters Libby and Marie and my daughter-in-law Sherry. Libby, a Spanish professor, often has students who want to get by with as little work as possible. Her first instinct, like mine, is to let them hang themselves and to fail as many as possible. After all, they are adults! But inevitably the anger energizes her to think more creatively about the content and pedagogy of the course, and about how to win the students' hearts and minds. Likewise Marie has faced the frustration of teaching junior high students whose emotional—not to mention physical—changes disrupt their lives and Marie's classroom. They can make you angry by simply shuffling into the room with that snarly look on their face. Marie had to learn how to transform her daily frustrations with these no-longer-children-and-not-yet-adults into constructive ways to learn to become more fully human. Sherry faces the same frustrations with the elementary children she teaches, not to mention their parents. Kathy and I have listened to tirades about lazy students, classmates being vicious toward each other, and parents who protect their children from the frustrations and joys of learning. But we have also listened to Sherry's phone conversations with her mother (Carol, like Sherry, is a master teacher) and have overheard these two gifted women transform anger into lesson plans and strategies that enabled Sherry to return with a fresh vision for her students.

## Speaking Our Anger in Love

But what about that third kind of anger, indignation, that so easily expresses itself in self-righteous, destructive words and acts that forever damage relationships? For this kind of anger to be good anger requires spiritual disciplines—the kind that Martin Luther King Jr. describes in "Letter from Birmingham Jail," which he wrote while in jail for protesting segregation in Birmingham, Alabama. He wrote in response to some white clergymen who scolded him as an "outside agitator" who lacked patience. His response is prophetic and eloquent. At one point he asserts, "I cannot sit idly by in Atlanta and not be concerned about what happens in Birmingham." He adds, "Injustice anywhere is a threat to justice everywhere." He goes on to explain why the demonstrations they so deplored were absolutely necessary. King reminds them that his commitment to nonviolence does not mean he will not confront injustice forcefully, without violence. He then describes the four basic steps of a nonviolent campaign: "collection of the facts to determine whether injustice exists; negotiation; self-purification; and direct action."[3] It seems to me that these steps describe a spiritual discipline that each of us could follow before expressing righteous indignation. Too often we become indignant before we know all the facts. Knowing the facts, we don't practice "speaking the truth in love" by trying to discuss the facts with the offending party. And if we feel we must confront a person with moral indignation— direct action—we must prayerfully reflect on our own lives and be willing to take violence on ourselves without retaliating violently, remembering that words can be an act of violence. For even the most ruthless perpetrator of injustice and violence against the innocent is beloved by God and redeemable—for example, Saul of Tarsus.

### Fire and Ice

By meeting those rare people who seem unable to feel or express anger, I have come to realize over the years that anger can be good. I once had a student who lied and cheated. When confronted about it, he was utterly placid. You could call him anything you liked, and he showed no emotional reaction. This is often the response of a sociopath: a person who has no conscience. This is probably why in his *Divine Comedy* Dante depicts the pit of hell where the worst sinners exist not as fire but ice. Anger can be a human and humanizing passion. But anger should be focused on the actions of specific persons and expressed in a timely way; in other words, it should not be generalized to whole groups of people who belong to the same race, class, gender, or authority structure as does the offending party. Once we know the facts, search our hearts, and pray, we should not delay expressing our anger—to be angry like Jesus.

This leads to my final thought. The Scriptures—Job, Psalms, the Prophets, Jesus's question to God from the cross—give us permission and even words to express our anger at God and to God. Jesus, as we know, quoted Psalm 22 from the cross: "My God, my God, why have you forsaken me?" Indeed, if we are worried about our anger spilling over into sinful fury, the example of Jesus would suggest that we should take our anger to God, who is not fragile and who understands that we are all children, like the ones whom Jesus took in his arms, anger and all.

## Questions

1. How did anger function and affect your family as you were growing up?
2. Do you find it hard to think of anger as good? If so, why?
3. What relationships in your life cause you the most frustration? How do you deal with it?
4. Have you ever experienced harnessed anger used effectively by your parents, teachers, or someone else in authority? Have you ever used such harnessed anger?
5. Can you share an experience from your own life of righteous indignation, when you feel you are being angry with God about an injustice in the world? Have you ever expressed anger to God about what seems to be his failure to be there for you or others?

# 10

## When Jesus Questioned the Father

### *How Doubt and Fear Drive Us to God*

> We don't quite dare walk between the flames,
> trusting that God can guide us and deliver us. We
> refuse to admit of tension and ambiguity. Because
> of that we can't honestly ask with the Psalmist,
> "Why, O Lord?"
>
> William Edgar[1]

One of my most vivid memories of the power of fear and doubt happened when I was on a plane that was landing in New Haven, Connecticut. I was on the way to a conference with two friends. We had managed to sit together from Dallas to New York, but we were seated next to strangers during the short commute from New York to New Haven. The woman seated next to me was a

well-dressed professional and an engaging conversational-
ist. I asked her about her work and learned, among other
things, that her profession demanded weekly plane travel.
I confessed my admiration for anyone who could face the
demands of such travel every week, letting her know that I
was not crazy about flying and considered it a heavy travel
year if I flew more than two or three times. She assured me
that you get accustomed to it and learn to use the plane as
your office. Realizing that I was sincere about not caring
to fly, she kindly warned me that we were about to land at
New Haven and often the landings across the water into
the airport are a bit choppy. She went on to assure me that
it usually isn't all that bad and, besides, this commuter
airline had the best pilots and equipment. She then went
on to say that she felt much safer, and indeed statistically is
much safer, in the air than on the freeways of Connecticut
and New York. I appreciated her sympathy and her logic.
My palms were only slightly sweaty as the pilot announced
to prepare for landing.

Sure enough, the choppiness started, but I was fore-
warned about this phenomenon and felt a renewed sense of
confidence and security with my new friend accompanying
me. Then it happened. We hit an air pocket and went from
chop to thud; the plane shook so that we looked like rag
dolls strapped in our seats. But most startling, my travel
companion grabbed my hand as if I were saving her from
falling over a ledge, broke into a cold sweat, and would
not let go until we felt the wheels touch ground. All of that
sophisticated cool and logical assurance was gone in a flash.
She was terrified and panic-stricken. She looked embar-

rassed when we landed, but I assured her that I was holding on to her hand as tightly as she was holding mine.

### Reason to Fear

What is fear? What is doubt? How can they be experienced in ways that make us more fully human? In what sense did Jesus fear and doubt, and how do his experiences of these alarming realities enable us to respond like him?

Fear in the biblical sense includes a range of meanings. At the more positive end is "the fear of the Lord," which can mean reverence and respect but includes a healthy sense of being afraid of a righteous God who is judge as well as redeemer. In this sense, Jesus and all who follow him fear the Lord: reverence, respect, and obey. Fear can also enslave a person and is, in this sense, the result of living in a fallen world. Indeed, systems of slavery, be they the old chattel slavery by which whites victimized blacks in this country or terrorist movements by which extremists victimize anyone who will not submit to their version of a religion or ideology, are built on systemic fear. A vivid example of this is depicted in Aleksandr Solzhenitsyn's novel *The First Circle*. He describes the Soviet bureaucrats in Moscow who would stay up all night, fearing that Stalin would call them for information or summon them to his office. They knew what he would do to anyone who failed to respond immediately. Even those at the highest echelon of power in this ruthless regime lived in fear day and night.[2] Finally, fear can be defined as sheer terror, as my travel companion and I experienced as nature rattled our fragile vessel and our self-possessed façade. Fear is visceral because we live in dying bodies in a dangerous world. We have reason to fear.

## Fear and Doubt

Doubt often follows fear, because when our reasoned composure is rattled by real or perceived danger, when our bodies shake and our palms sweat, we cannot help but call into question our neat and tidy explanations of the way things appear to be. This is the conflict described in the book of Job. Job and his friends believe that good things happen to good people and bad things happen to bad people. When Job's afflictions begin, neither he nor his friends have any way of explaining what is really going on. So they retreat to their tidy theology that leads to only one conclusion—Job has sinned. Job agrees with that theology, but he knows he has not sinned and does not deserve the suffering that afflicts him. He does not propose a new theological system; he simply pleads with God to vindicate him. Neither Job nor his friends ever mention Satan, the accuser, so that all good and evil in human experience find their source, according to their theology, in humans or in God. In the end, God does vindicate Job and accuses his accusers. The book of Job does not replace the pious and simplistic theology of Job and his accusers with a new system but with a revelation, a story of God who boasts on his creatures and who longs to restore them, but in the meantime permits the mystery of human suffering. Job had reason to fear and reason to doubt, but both his fear and doubt drove him into the arms of God and to seek God's justification of him.

While Job did not commit sins that caused his tragic losses, he was a sinner, so we would expect him to experience fear and doubt. But Jesus was not a sinner, so why would he who always obeyed his Father ever fear, except in the sense of reverencing the Father? Why would he ever doubt the Father's word or the Spirit's leading? While we can understand that Jesus could be fully God and still experience anger, how could he experience fear and doubt? If he did, in what sense are we to understand this?

### Jesus's Fear and Doubt

To my way of thinking and reading Scripture, Jesus experienced fear and doubt only in Gethsemane and on the cross. Even though he was tempted by Satan in the wilderness, caught in a storm at sea, verbally assaulted by the Jewish leaders, or standing before Herod and Pilate, Jesus expressed fear and doubt only in the garden pleading with the Father and on the cross crying out to him. Why then and not before?

Physically, he was about to die. Certainly he had faced a mysterious transformation in the incarnation: true God becoming true humanity. But that was divine life taking on human life. This would be the one who said "I am the way and the truth and the life" (John 14:6) becoming death for us. Nor was he facing this anticipatory grief as a sinful human being, like you and me. "When you eat of it [the forbidden tree], you will surely die" (Gen. 2:17) is not only God's judgment on Adam and Eve; it is a judgment we carry in our body, mind, and spirit. We know in the depths of ourselves that something in us is dying, and we experience little deaths all of our lives, whether from critical illness, alienation from family and friends, broken hearts, broken minds, and broken spirits, or from all the final good-byes we must say to those we love. We who are sinners are caught in the mortality game, so long as we are separated from the source of our lives.

### Driven by Fear

Jesus, until that night in the garden, was not living such little deaths, because he knew that the Father was with him and he with the Father, who delighted in him. There was nothing in the cells of his body, in the thoughts and memories of his mind, or in the longing of his spirit that deserved or embodied death. For him to face death was a fearful prospect that drove him that night into the arms of the Father, asking for this cup of undeserved suffering to pass from him; but he confessed, above all, he wanted to do the Father's will.

While the Gospel writers describe this as a deeply emotional event, Luke, the physician, adds, "An angel from heaven appeared to him and strengthened him" (22:43). We recall that the message of the angels at Jesus's birth began, "Fear not!" But Luke does not record such a word from this angel. Indeed, we are told immediately after the angel strengthened him, "Being in anguish, he prayed more earnestly, and his sweat was like drops of blood falling to the ground" (22:44). Whether we take this as literal hematidrosis—the actual mingling of blood and sweat—or as a comparison of Jesus's sweat with blood, we must face the fact that his very body was suffering fear. This fear drove him to his knees, to plead like the psalmists with the

Father, to open his fearful and trembling self to the God from whom he had never known separation.

## God-Forsaken

Then came the dark hour when Jesus faced the mystery that was at the heart of his sacrifice on the cross. I don't pretend to understand or explain the exchange that went on between the Father and the Son. The Gospels simply tell us that after Jesus had suffered the cruel torture of the cross for several hours—with profound equanimity—he cried out in agony to the Father in the words of Psalm 22: "My God, my God, why have you forsaken me?" Just as fear had driven him to the Father's presence in the garden, so his doubt drove him to the Word of God. I agree with those Christian teachers through the ages who believe that Jesus was crying out not only in agony because God could have saved him from torture and didn't; more profoundly, the Father was well pleased at his baptism, called Jesus beloved on the Mount of Transfiguration, but was unavailable to Jesus at any level of relationship, for any comfort, much less delight and love. St. Paul expresses the mystery of this God-forsaken moment in Jesus's life: "God made him who had no sin to be sin for us, so that in him we might become the righteousness of God" (2 Cor. 5:21). I cannot fathom such suffering, such love, both on the part of Jesus our Savior and on the part of God the Father and God the Spirit. Jesus was God-forsaken for us, so that we would never be God-forsaken.

Unlike anger, as we discussed in the last chapter, fear and doubt are less about doing than they are about being.

We live in a dangerous world, as the psalmist reminds us time and again, and we need someone to protect us, to keep us in the shadow of his wings, like the mother eagle does for her chicks in the nest. Jesus told his disciples not to fear anyone or anything but him; and fearing him, they had nothing to fear. But the fear of the Lord, the fear and doubt that lead us to his embrace and to his Word, often begin with threats to our lives and our relationships that could also drive us away from God and his Word. Jesus teaches us in the crucial moments of his fear and doubt that there is nothing wrong with fear, even fear that makes us sweat blood, and there is nothing wrong with expressing doubt, even shouting it from a cross in public. Such fear and doubt can deepen our relationship with God and our trust in God's Word, because we learn in these moments that God's love and God's Word can absorb and handle our visceral fears and our intellectual doubts.

### The Refuge of God's Embrace

What can we, who face clutching fears and who wrestle with doubt, learn from our Lord about living these human realities, and yet being without sin? First, we must embrace our fears and doubts as opportunities to be driven to God, to be honest with God, and to rest in God's embrace. Each time some danger arouses fear in us, we must remember that "perfect love casts out fear" (1 John 4:18), and only God has perfect love. We must learn that he delights in us, that we are beloved, just as Jesus was. Another way of expressing this is that we must be reminded in these moments of who stands behind us.

137

Let me illustrate what I mean by way of a story my wife, Kathy, told me when we both worked at a K–12 school. One day she drove our two sons to school, arriving shortly before classes started. Probably because they were cutting it close, she noticed a high school student tearing into the parking lot nearest the elementary school at a dangerous speed. She was so angry at this reckless young man who could have injured or killed a child that she got out of her car, marched over to him with our younger son Harry, leaving his older brother Will behind, poked her finger in the offender's muscular chest, and said, "Do you have any idea what you were doing? I never want to see you do such a thing again—never! Do you understand me?" The young man sheepishly said, "Yes, ma'am," and went to class. When she told me, I was impressed because Kathy is not usually that bold. She said that our gigantic son Will had positioned himself behind her. Jesus walked through life knowing that the Father went before and behind him.

## Finding a Hiding Place

Jesus also unashamedly took refuge in the Father. He knew the Psalms by heart and quoted them constantly; he took to heart one of their major themes: God is our refuge, our rock, and our hiding place. Human beings are vulnerable and needy; the world is sinful and dangerous. Fear is the alarm God has built into our bodies to remind us to take refuge in him. We can do so for other reasons: love, prayer, praise, and just abiding, hanging out in the presence of God. But when we fear and doubt, we are

138

reminded that taking refuge in him is not only a choice, it is necessary to our very sense of security and peace.

Finally, Jesus's life reminds us that if we will read and understand the Scriptures as they are written, we cannot escape the fact that the Bible is chock-full of expressions of fear and doubt to God. From the stories of Abraham and Sarah and the patriarchs and matriarchs who followed them to Job, Ecclesiastes, the Psalms, and the Prophets, men and women of authentic faith were audacious enough to cry out to God their fears and doubts, and God was audacious enough to include those outcries in his Word. Nor are these expressions of fear and doubt only in the Old Testament. The Gospels are replete with expressions of fear and doubt among the disciples, and the letters of the apostles speak to the countless fears and doubts of those in the early church. God is not fragile. God's Word is robust. Jesus teaches us in the most crucial moments in his life to express boldly our fears and doubts in the most crucial moments of our lives.

## Questions

1. What experiences in your life have so jarred you that you felt overwhelmed by fear?
2. When you or others have experienced a crisis of faith, have you found that family and friends try to comfort you with tidy explanations and pious platitudes? Give examples of some of these and why they do not comfort you.
3. Unlike Jesus, we are born in bodies that are destined to die because of our sinful nature, and we have

experienced separation from the Father. What difference can walking through our fears and doubts with Jesus make in our lives?

4. What does Jesus's cry, "My God, my God, why have you forsaken me?" mean to you?

5. Have you experienced fear and doubt that drove you to God's embrace? What did that experience do to your relationship with God?

# 11

## Extreme Jesus

### *Eschewing Stereotypical Spirituality*

See, from His head, His hands, His feet,
Sorrow and love flow mingled down;
Did e'er such love and sorrow meet,
Or thorns compose so rich a crown?

"When I Survey the Wondrous Cross"
by Isaac Watts

Many Christians and many churches participate in a kind of spiritual profiling; this profiling is not about ethnicity or color but personality type. It may vary from one denominational tradition to another. But in my experience, most American Christians see two kinds of personalities as spiritual or godly. First, especially for men, a spiritually mature person is phlegmatic: calm, even-tempered, and not given to emotional expression. In the face of triumph and tragedy, he is unflappable, no high fives and no tearful outbursts. He is a rock. The other personality type that is most often perceived as godly, especially among women, is the sanguine person: cheerful, confident, and optimistic. She always can see and will express the positive even in the midst of tragedy and suffering. She looks on the bright side of everything.

These spiritual stereotypes are dangerous for at least three reasons. First, Scripture does not teach that becoming spiritual homogenizes our personalities. It does teach that we are to love, be joyful, act kindly, and so forth. But a moody person or an edgy person can love, be joyful, and act kindly. Indeed, we might argue that a person who is not naturally sweet or calm may show more of the fruit of the Holy Spirit acting this way than the person who always appears to be nice. Nice is not always spiritual. In fact, nice and calm and sweet can be forms of denying reality and of refusing to connect at a deep level with the triumphs and tragedies of others.

Which leads to my second reason for saying stereotypical spirituality is dangerous. When we recall some of the godliest men and women described in the Bible—Abraham and Sarah, Moses, Deborah, David, Isaiah, Peter, and Paul—they are anything but calm and sweet. These and many other spiritually mature men and women are edgy, emotional, melancholic, fervent, and outspoken, including of course Jesus Christ. He wept, laughed, loved children, scorned religious hypocrites, and angrily drove pious thieves from the temple. But we will take this up later.

My final reason for describing this religious profiling as dangerous is that people who are always phlegmatic and sanguine are usually in denial or, worse yet, exploiting others with their winsome personalities. An example of denial that comes to mind is that of a friend whose six-year-old son died in an accident. This friend was a Christian leader who believed firmly and rightly that his child was with Jesus. He believed it so fervently that he calmly counseled and comforted those of us who were weeping in our grief over this tragic loss. He, in fact, was the main speaker at the memorial service. Few of us had ever witnessed such a triumphant trust in the face of such a loss; it was beyond us. And, in reality, it was beyond him, for almost a year later he went into deep grief and depression. He worked through it, by the grace of God and with the help of his wife and children, but he would later confess that he had refused to grieve.

Far worse than putting on a pious face to cope with the death of child is the Christian leader who exploits others with his victorious and always positive faith. I need not name any particular person, since most of us can think of too many. Much of the television church industry and many Christian radio programs are given to this exploitation. They bring on guest after guest who share their triumphs in faith, while being interviewed by a phlegmatic male preacher whose sanguine wife or female cohost gazes admiringly at him, occasionally saying something sweet and positive. Whether we are told explicitly or simply infer it, the strong impression is that we too can become a triumphant Christian, exuding spiritual calm and sweetness, especially if we send money.

## Grief to Joy

Jesus was not stoic, smooth, sweet, or emotionless. His response to little children, the sick, the poor, and those who struggled with life was neither *"c'est la vie"* nor "I wonder what God wants to teach you through these hardships." Jesus entered into the joys of others—"a friend of tax collectors and 'sinners'" (Matt. 11:19)—and he felt deeply the suffering of others, whether weeping at Lazarus's tomb or grieving over Jerusalem. In his humanity he embraced the extremes of life, its joys and its sorrows, witnessing to a way of being passionate and compassionate. Indeed, in him we witness a way of being human that is open to feeling deeply for and with our loved ones, our neighbors, strangers, and enemies. Jesus understood joy and sorrow as gifts from God that enable us to experience life's highs and lows with grace and passion.

I have alluded to a number of incidents in the life of Jesus when he expresses joy and sorrow, openly and without shame. But I think no occasion in his life better reveals the depth of his passion than the evening he shared the last Passover and first communion meal with his disciples. We should not forget that the Passover meal itself serves as a remembrance for Jews of their bitter suffering and sorrows in Egypt and of their joyful liberation from slavery in Egypt. They not only remembered with their minds and words, they remembered with the smells and tastes of joy mixed with sorrow. Knowing this, Jesus uses this occasion to express to his disciples his joy and his Father's joy in them. He washes their feet as a genuine expression of his love and affection, as well as an example to them of how they are to love each other.

Knowing that Judas is a betrayer, Jesus is "deeply troubled" that one of his disciples, his friend, would betray him. He compares their intimate connection to the organic union of a vine and a branch. Building on this image, he then teaches them that the first fruit of their union is that they obey the new commandment he gives them: "Love each other as I have loved you" so that "my joy may be in you and that your joy may be complete" (John 15:11–12). These are not only the words but also the deeply felt affections of his love for them spoken with abandon.

### The Promise of Sorrow and Hate

Having said this, he warns them that they will also face great sorrow—the world will hate them as it hates him. Having taught them about love beyond imagination and hate beyond reason, Jesus, feeling their grief, assures them that the Holy Spirit will counsel and comfort them when he is gone. He lets them know that he knows they grieve and, at his death, will grieve while the world that murders him rejoices. But, he reassures them, "Your grief will turn to joy" (John 16:20–33), just as a woman giving birth forgets the pain when her baby is born. He does not tell them that there will be no pain or that pain is an illusion; indeed, he tells them, "In this world you will have trouble." "But take heart!" he says. "I have overcome the world." These are not the pious words of a righteous rabbi, a stoic guru, or a phlegmatic optimist. These are the words of the one the prophets called "a man of sorrows and familiar with suffering" (Isa. 53:3), who would pass through hate, torture, execution, hell, and resurrection to turn their grief to joy. He knew that through the Passover meal, the first communion, and his teachings that evening, he expressed more joy and sorrow than his disciples could bear at one time. The Spirit would have to teach them the rest, after his death and resurrection, and through the joys and griefs that they were to experience.

I understand why we fragile human beings want to shut down our feelings. We feel like F. Scott Fitzgerald's Nick Carraway in *The Great Gatsby*. Having witnessed the death of Gatsby and the brokenness of the debauched crowd he ran with, Nick declares, "When I came back from the East last autumn I felt that I wanted the world to be in uniform and at a sort of moral attention forever; I wanted no more riotous excursions with privileged glimpses into the human heart."[1] Nick risked caring about these riotous people, and that risk caused him unspeakable suffering. His response to that pain was to run away and pretend he could escape it altogether. It is dangerous to enter boldly into life's joys and sorrow. Love demands that we remove our protective armor, that we drop our defensive guards, and that we feel deeply with and for each other. But when the armor is in place, the guard is up, and we refuse to love, we also refuse to live life fully, as Jesus dared to do and as he taught his disciples to do as well.

## Our Glorious and Fallen World

Life is a pain; life is joy. Jesus entered into both extremes of life, enlarging our vision, even in a fallen world, of the glories of being human. He engaged with people at every level, fully entering into their lives, fully feeling their emotions, without emotionalism or manipulation. With him and through him we are called to experience the fullness of our humanity, to grieve with those who grieve and to rejoice with those who rejoice. The stoic and the phlegmatic in us tell us not to celebrate the joys of life, because the wheel of fate will turn. Sorrows will come. Likewise, they would say that since life ends in death and joy always gives way to sorrow, keep a stiff upper lip and don't give in to grief. The optimist and the sanguine in us would tell us not to grieve, because it will all turn out okay in the end, that we will live happily ever after, and that the sorrows are not real. Jesus feared neither joy nor sorrow; he knew that to love God and to love our neighbor is to embrace their joys and sorrows. To refuse to do so is not only to refuse to be fully human as he was, but to refuse to keep risking love with our spouses until death parts us, to keep loving our children through their successes and failures, to love our neighbors in their celebrations and losses, and finally to love our glorious and fallen world.

### Eating Our Sorrow

Every time Christians around the world share communion, we participate body, soul, and spirit in the joys and sorrows of Jesus. For at that table we remember his broken body, his agony, and his abandonment. We call it celebrating communion, and part of what we celebrate is unspeakable sorrow. Yet we also celebrate his resurrection, his glorification, and his coming again. In doing so we not only confess our sins, we also confess our redeemed humanity by participating in his humanity, body and blood.

We do so around a meal, that most human of experiences, and one that reminds us of our dependence on God, one another, and God's good earth.

Jesus understood then and understands now that to enter into such joy and such sorrow is more than we can bear alone. He never asks us to bear it alone. In our God-given and Christ-redeemed humanity we are given the gifts of sorrow and joy that free us from protecting ourselves, that free us to give ourselves, that free us to experience God's passion for us and to embody God's passion for the world.

### Questions

1. What is your profile or ideal of a spiritually mature Christian?
2. Have you (or anyone else) felt misunderstood by Christians, because they did not find you acceptable or mature?
3. Does your tradition fall into spiritual profiling and, if so, does it agree with what is described in this chapter or is it a different stereotype?
4. Have you experienced privately or in a community these experiences of joy and sorrow mixed? Describe the experience.
5. Are there relationships or opportunities you hesitate to experience, because they will almost certainly bring great joy and sorrow? What would it mean to enter those with Jesus?

# 12

## How Should Christians Die?

### *A Lesson in the End of Life*

Unreal City,
Under the Brown Fog of a winter dawn,
A crowd flowed over London Bridge, so many,
I had not thought death had undone so many.

T. S. Eliot[1]

## Death: A Scandal and an Offense

Death is a scandal to humanity and an offense to God. We
are told in Genesis that death was not part of God's original
design, that it originated when the first human beings tried
to trade their humanity for divinity. Human pride and envy
brought death into creation, because once human beings
chose to be independent of God, we also chose to separate
ourselves from the source of life. So when we say we live in
a fallen world, we mean that it was not created for death,
but life; we were created to live forever, not to die. But die
we must. I first learned this not in Sunday school but sitting

with my father while he held his mother's hand and prayed over her as she lay dying in a hospital room. I was only a boy with little to no understanding of death. But I knew that my grandmother, who had come late to faith in Christ after living a hard and immoral life, was not passing away but was passing on. I knew that old body, which had finally failed her, was not her. I knew that my father's task was to accompany her as far as he could on that lonely journey, and then let her cross over. It has taken me another fifty years of living and witnessing scores of family and friends make that crossing to understand the theological reason why death is so scandalous and yet hope is so real.

My experience as a young boy in that hospital room reminds me of C. S. Lewis describing the day he heard about the sudden death of his friend Charles Williams. They were close friends, congenial colleagues, and Williams had as much influence as anyone on Lewis becoming a Christian and cultivating a Christian imagination. Lewis had heard that Williams was in the hospital, and he was going to visit him when he heard that Williams had passed on. He describes walking back home, bewildered by the news. "When the idea of death and the idea of Williams . . . met in my mind, it was the idea of death that was changed."[2] Nothing in the nature of things would cause us to think that a dead body is not a dead person, and yet we know in the depths of us that this beloved person is not to be equated with this dead body.

## Born to Die

While death is said to be "natural" to us fallen creatures, it was not natural to Jesus. He did not sin; he surely should not die. He was, as no other human being, a life force. His touch healed the sick, his blessing on food fed thousands, and his words calmed storms and raised the dead. He exuded life; his very presence was life-giving. How could death touch him? Why? And yet at the heart of the mystery of God's love for creation is the death of Jesus. Likewise, at the heart of Christian worship from the first Christians to the contemporary church is communion, when we partake of his broken body and his spilled blood. Christians sing, pray, and preach about the death of Christ and the death of his followers. From the earliest hymns and creeds of the church fathers through the Middle Ages and Reformation to the contemporary church, we Christians sing about death—his death and our deaths: "Beneath the Cross of Jesus," "Go to Dark Gethsemane," "O Sacred Head, Now Wounded," "When I Survey the Wondrous Cross," "Alas! And Did My Savior Bleed," "Were You There When They Crucified My Lord," "The Old Rugged Cross," and so on. We adorn our sanctuaries, our homes, and our bodies with crucifixes and crosses. We believe, as no other religion, that Jesus was truly God and truly human, that his death and resurrection has forever transformed death into a symbol of eternal life—ours through his.

## Fatalists and Dreamers

This idea of death transformed by Jesus is folly to much of our modern scientific world, which tells us two different lies about death and dying. The first is that the material world is all there is, that it and we are insignificant specks on an obscure planet, dying with it. This death is perfectly natural, we are told. We pass away, or pass into some other form of matter or energy. As American poet e. e. cummings expresses this view in his cynical celebration of a dying world: "when god lets my body be/ from each brave eye will sprout a tree."[3] In other words, human beings are born to die; after that we are compost. This is still the dominant view of most people who believe that humans are highly evolved matter—nothing more. Those who hold this view are the pessimistic, or they would say realistic, materialists.

Over the past thirty years a second lie has been created by a small but elite group of scientific materialists who are more optimistic and idealistic. We gain a glimpse into the current state of their thinking through an article written by Bill Joy, chief scientist at Sun Microsystems, in *Wired Magazine* entitled "Why the Future Doesn't Need Us." It opens with Joy's confession of knowledge without wisdom:

> From the moment I became involved in the creation of new technologies, their ethical dimensions have concerned me, but it was only in the autumn of 1998 that I became anxiously aware of how great are the dangers facing us in the 21st century. I can date the onset of my unease to the day I met Ray Kurzweil, the deservedly famous inventor of the first reading machine for the blind and many other amazing things.[4]

He then goes on to tell how he had missed Kurzweil's paper at this conference, so later he sat with another friend to discuss it. He was shocked to hear "Ray saying that the rate of improvement of technology was going to accelerate and that we were going to become robots or fuse (half robot/half human) with robots or something like that."[5] Here was an eminent scientist saying that as early as 2030, we could have technologies that would allow us to download our brains into sentient, intelligent, possibly self-replicating robots. Kurzweil gave Joy a partial reprint of his then-forthcoming book *The Age of Spiritual Machines*, "which outlined a utopia he foresaw—one in which humans gained near immortality by becoming one with robotic technology."[6] Some secular scientists would have us resign ourselves to becoming compost while others fantasize our becoming techno-immortals.

### Seven Words of Real Hope

Jesus's death presents us with a realism that is not resignation, with a hope that does not annihilate our humanity. Knowing that he was passing through death to resurrection, Jesus was able to face the hard realities of dying with a human and humanizing faith, hope, and love. These are evident in all four Gospel narratives of his suffering and death, but especially in the so-called "seven words from the cross," a composite of his final utterances recorded variously in the Gospels. From these words spoken while he was slowly dying, we may learn how to die with grace, with him.

He first prays, "Father, forgive them, for they do not know what they are doing" (Luke 23:34). While the most obvious people he has in mind are those who unjustly condemned, tortured, and are now crucifying him, he could equally be praying for the disciples who deserted him and

153

the crowd who earlier in the week threw palm leaves at his feet. He must seek the Father's forgiveness of them, because the temptation when we think we are dying is to either become bitter at those who have the audacity to keep on living or to settle scores with those who have wronged, abused, or neglected us. Jesus, the dying human, gives them over to the grace and love of God.

Next he responds compassionately to one of the criminals who pleads, "Jesus, remember me when you come into your kingdom." Jesus replies, "I tell you the truth, today you will be with me in paradise" (Luke 23:42–43). Jesus graces a fellow human being with complete acceptance, not asking him to repent and do penance; the thief knows that he is receiving his just punishment, while Jesus is a victim of injustice, including that from the other criminal who mocks Jesus along with the mob of spectators.

John records the third word that Jesus "said to his mother, 'Dear woman, here is your son' and to the disciple, 'Here is your mother'" (John 19:26–27). Here Jesus attends to his responsibility to Mary, his mother and faithful disciple. He knows, like all dying people know, that he will leave a hole in the lives of those closest to him, those most dependent on him. Like any good Jew, like any good human being, he must honor his mother to the end—her end or his end. His present suffering and his future resurrection do not excuse him from honoring and attending to these intimate relationships and practical concerns.

Having committed his mother to John's care, as they stood at the foot of the cross, he cries out to his Father, "My God, my God, why have you forsaken me?" (Matt. 27:46). What a shocking contrast: his earthly mother stands at the foot of the cross; his heavenly Father has forsaken him. As we discussed earlier, the mystery here, as best we can understand it, is expressed in Paul's explanation: "God made him who had no sin to be sin for us" (2 Cor. 5:21). I take this to mean that while Jesus could not sin and separate himself from the Father, the Father and the Spirit separated themselves from him, so that he would experience the alienation that sin produces in human beings, having done nothing to alienate himself. He was God-forsaken in some sense and, like the psalmist whose words he utters, was free to cry out in the anguish of his abandonment.

John then records his brief expression of physical suffering, "I am thirsty" (John 19:28). He has been bleeding for hours and hanging in the scorching sun; he longs for the physical taste of liquid. He wants the comfort of that sponge soaked in wine vinegar, knowing that he is about to yield to death; his body in all its glorious tortured humanity wants to quench his thirst one more time before he lets go.

John then tells us that after Jesus receives the wine, he says, "It is finished." Whether he knew it in his flesh and bones or because the Father had told him, he had done his work, he had finished his mission, he had yielded himself completely to God's will and to our good in this life. He was ready to let go.

We are told his final words, like his first, were spoken to the Father, but now in a loud voice, as he crosses the finish line: "Father, into your hands I commit my spirit" (Luke 23:46). What happens as he passes on into the Father's hands is a mystery, as it will be for each of us. What we

155

do know is that the next time we see him he inhabits a resurrected body.

## He Loved the World to Death

There are those who would say that all of this talk and teaching about resurrection, the next world, and the kingdom of God diminishes the value of this life, this world. I agree that this has been a problem throughout the history of the church: self-flagellating forms of monasticism, world-hating forms of Puritanism, and time-escaping forms of millennialism. But these have nothing to do with following Jesus in his life, death, and resurrection. He loved this world. He begged the Father, if it were possible, not to go through the terrors of the crucifixion. Indeed, in his public life he was accused of partying with publicans and sinners, of dining with tax collectors and prostitutes, of eating and drinking more than becomes a rabbi or a prophet. He loved even his enemies from the cross. He loved a criminal on the cross. He loved his mother and his disciples, as they stood by helplessly. He loved that final taste of wine vinegar. He loved them all to death.

## Jesus Kills Death

Death is our enemy. It reminds us we are sinners and not long for this world for which we long. The death of Jesus is no pious and simple answer to the questions raised by death. It deepens the questions, because God saw fit to participate in our humanity even to the point of dying on a cross. Death still has a sting, and it will until Christ kills death in his coming again. But in the meantime, we should grieve the passing of those we love and feel free to grieve deeply. I have learned this not only from Jesus and the psalms he so often quoted, but from my wife. Kathy feels deeply for people and for God. I realized this most vividly when we heard the news many years ago that our two-year-old nephew, Bart, was killed in a car accident. We both cried for days, grieving for the passing of this beautiful young life and for the unspeakable grief his death brought to his parents. Kathy found it particularly difficult because it was Easter season. That nature and the church would celebrate life in the face of Bart's death seemed unfeeling and unbearable. In her grief, she gave her expression to her love in a poem, remembering how Bart loved to swing in the backyard:

> Behind the high hedge you would swing
> > Fair-haired boy of my innocence
> > Now I see you
> > Now I don't
> > And now I don't again
>
> You flew away
> > Dressed up for all the world like a party had begun.
> > Lord, Lord, how the images lie.

The death of someone we love should fill us with grief. The Scripture is not sentimental or pious about death and dying, nor was Jesus. He came to live a fully human life; he died a fully human death. His body succumbed, as will our own. But death could not prevent him from loving his

Father, his mother, his enemies, his betrayers, his deniers, his mockers, and even that last taste of wine. Because he was willing to die unjustly and God-forsaken, we can die like him but with him.

## Questions

1. When you were growing up, what was your experience and understanding of death and dying?
2. What symptoms do you see in our culture of people denying or avoiding death?
3. Which of the last seven words of Jesus most speak to your questions and concerns about death?
4. What can his seven words from the cross teach us about the process of letting go, whether in the deaths of others or in our own death?
5. How do we learn from Jesus to enter into our grief, to truly grieve our griefs and not merely have grief overwhelm us?

# 13

## Scarred for Life

### *The Stories Our Wounds Tell*

Then he kept still, while the old nurse filled up
her basin glittering in firelight; she poured
cold water in, then hot.
But Lord Odysseus
whirled suddenly from the fire to face the dark.
The scar: he had forgotten that. She must not
Handle his scarred thigh, or the game was up.

Homer, *The Odyssey*[1]

Scars remember and reveal much about our lives. We learn this from literature, from Scripture, and from our personal stories. One of the most vivid examples from the stories we have traditionally read in school comes from Homer's *Odyssey*. As you may recall from high school English class, this is the story of a kingdom in crisis, because King Odysseus has been away at war for almost twenty years. His wife Penelope is besieged by suitors who assume her husband is dead, the royal palace has become a hangout for debauched young aristocrats to party and exploit royal hospitality, and Prince Telemachus has grown up without a father to love and guide him. Everyone knows that the Trojan War, which caused Odysseus to leave, has been over for ten years, so they understandably assume that he is dead and that the queen, for the sake of Ithaca, should remarry.

In the meantime, shipwrecked and wretched, Odysseus is very much alive and trying to return home. He finally conspires with his son and his father to return in disguise, so that the suitors won't try to kill him and the royal family before he can avenge their honor. He comes home disguised as a beggar, and no one recognizes him, not even his wife—no one, except his old nursemaid. When she is asked to wash the feet of this stranger as an act of hospitality, this woman who has known him from boyhood is completely deceived until she sees the old wound on his thigh. That scar does not lie; Odysseus received it from the attack of a wild boar while on a hunting trip. She cannot forget the story of a wound that recalls the courage of the lord she has served so long. He convinces her to reveal this to no one, because he must surprise those who have violated his family and hospitality, or they will kill him and his family. This episode from the *Odyssey* dramatizes how our bodies remember what our minds and hearts forget.

## Scars Remember

Scars are crucial memorials that mark our crises and turning points. As I type these words on my computer, I look down at my fifty-eight-year-old hands, which are slowly revealing scars that I had forgotten: the inch-long scar on my left wrist with the pencil lead color still visible. In junior high I stuck my pencil in my pocket and forgot that it was there until later, when showing off in front of my friends. I jammed my hands in my jeans pockets, and out came my wrist with a no. 2 pencil dangling from it! (I will not even discuss the pencil wound from when Jimmy put a pencil under me as I sat down at my desk.) When I look in the mirror, my face reveals the scar on my lower lip from when I slipped on the ice and my tooth bit through my lip. Recently, I recalled my appendicitis operation when I was ten years old; my appendix burst as they were taking it out. I spent two weeks in the hospital while they fought the infection and two more weeks at home recovering.

The reason I recently recalled that surgery is because I am accompanying Kathy through the difficult journey of early-stage breast cancer, two surgeries, chemotherapy and radiation treatments. As I have watched her face this harsh reality with authentic faith in Jesus and with her amazing sense of humor intact, I have recalled the other scars she has borne during our thirty-seven years together: the emergency D&C after Marie's birth, when she almost bled to death as I drove to the hospital at over one hundred miles per hour; her car accident, which she still does not remember, when she was cut out of the car and careflighted to the hospital, where she spent eleven days followed by two months of recovery; her hysterectomy five years later;

and now the cancer surgery. All these make her beautiful body a living memorial to God's faithfulness, her offering of her body as a living sacrifice to God, and the great gift of family and friends who have embraced us time and again with prayer and love. Her scars participate in the love of Jesus and transform painful experiences into grace-filled memories and signs of hope.

### Resurrecting Scars

I linger introducing the power and significance of our scars in order to reflect with you on the extraordinary significance of the scars that marked Jesus's body, before and after the resurrection. We have discussed from a number of perspectives the mystery that God became flesh and dwelt among us, even to the point of dying the death of a common criminal. Yet as we discussed in the last chapter, death was defeated in the resurrection of Jesus. But why then are we told that his resurrected body was also scarred with the wounds of crucifixion and the piercing of his side with a spear? There are those who would like to say that we should not take the resurrection so literally. But that is the way the Scriptures describe it, and what does it mean to take it any other way?

As Paul asserts in New Testament theology: "If there is no resurrection from the dead, then not even Christ has been raised. And if Christ has not been raised, our preaching is useless and so is your faith" (1 Cor. 15:13–14). New Testament faith is resurrection faith. It is not about Jesus of Nazareth dying and leaving disciples who finally got it, spiritually speaking. It is about men and women who saw their risen Lord Jesus and believed so completely that large numbers of them suffered and died to spread the Good News. As New Testament scholar N. T. Wright has written in response to those who assert that resurrection meant something spiritual or psychological to the early Christians:

> The word resurrection was only used to describe reembodiment, not the state of disembodied bliss. Resurrection was not a general word for "life after death" or for "going to be with God" in some general sense. It was the word for what happened when God created newly embodied human beings after whatever intermediate state [after death] there might be.[2]

He goes on to say in here and other works that Christians do not believe in immortal souls but in resurrected bodies—transformed embodied selves. If we take seriously that Jesus died and rose again in a body and promised that we will do the same, then perhaps we can begin to understand what Paul means in this same passage when he writes these wonderfully mysterious words: "There are also heavenly bodies and there are earthly bodies; but the splendor of the heavenly bodies is one kind, and the splendor of the earthly bodies is another" (1 Cor. 15:40). I will not pretend to explain the full meaning of Paul's words, but I do want to suggest two insights. First, Paul says that both forms of embodied humanity, earthly and heavenly, are splendid, or if you wish, glorious: two different kinds of glory. I would add to this the observation that Jesus lived in both kinds of glorious bodies—with scars.

## Touching Jesus's Scars

In Jesus, the scars we bear, both physically and psychologically ("My God, my God, why . . . ?") define much of who we are, and Jesus's scars, which are by grace our scars, reveal something about embracing our gloriously scarred humanity. Nowhere is this disturbing and encouraging revelation more evident than in John's telling of the doubting of Thomas.

Most of us know the story of "doubting Thomas," who missed the first post-resurrection appearance of Jesus and could not make himself believe that Jesus was alive. Thomas is more than a skeptic; he has given his life to Jesus and seen him arrested, tortured, executed, and dead. Thomas has a questioning mind and a broken heart. He will not give himself to an illusion or a dream. Or, as he puts it, "Unless I see the nail marks in his hands and put my fingers where the nails were, and put my hand into his side, I will not believe it" (John 20:25). Eight days later Jesus meets his demand. Preachers and theologians for two millennia have probed and pondered the meanings of this encounter. But the Italian Renaissance artist Caravaggio captures it poignantly in his shocking painting *The Incredulity of St. Thomas.* New Testament theologian and art lover Walter Hansen describes Caravaggio's disturbing interpretation of this picture:

> Jesus places his hand on the arm of Thomas and gently, firmly guides that dirty hand into himself. As you look closely at the eyes of the other two disciples, you see that they are looking with utter amazement at the hand of Jesus guiding the hand of Thomas. The hand of the risen Lord guides the search.[3]

The wound in the side of Jesus is a passage to faith, an opening to grace. Hansen vividly describes Caravaggio's depiction of John's words, that Jesus did not hesitate to invite and guide Thomas to put his hand in Jesus's wound, to touch the mystery of his loving body that was pierced for us, and to begin to apprehend the beauty of the body wounded for love. Those wounds serve as memorials just as surely as communion memorializes his flesh in bread and wine. When, with Thomas, we dare to thrust our dirty hands into his wounds, we are reminded of his overwhelming love and grace. Indeed, he invites us to probe these wounds and to probe our own wounded humanity along with his suffering redemption. Better to do that than piously ignore his wounds and our own. For as Isaiah proclaims, "By his wounds we are healed" (Isa. 53:5).

## Scarred Glory

Our tendency, when we look at wounded humanity, others' or our own, is to avert our eyes and hope by doing so that we can make "the world to be in uniform and at a sort of moral attention forever." But we are wounded, and our scars show it. Yet, we are glorious, as C. S. Lewis reminds us:

> There are no *ordinary* people. You have never talked to a mere mortal. Nations, cultures, arts, civilizations—these are mortal, and their life is to ours as the life of a gnat. But it is immortals whom we joke with, work with, marry, snub, and exploit—immortal horrors or everlasting splendors. . . . Next to the Blessed Sacrament itself, your neighbor is the holiest object present to your senses.[4]

Like the blessed sacrament, these immortals that we call neighbors represent, each in his or her own way, broken bodies and scarred lives. Jesus's scarred, resurrected body startles and surprises us, because it tells us that the scars, which mark our immortal lives in the splendor of this earthly body, will be transformed into an even greater splendor to mark the beauty of our resurrected bodies.

## Scars That Tell Our Stories

I can only vaguely understand the implications of these glorious scars that help map our stories, just as I only vaguely understand the glory of the resurrected body of Jesus. But let me suggest a few directions for what Jesus teaches us about our scarred lives. First, the fact that our scars can become a redemptive part of our lives does not diminish the pain and horrors that caused them, just as Christians remember through Lent and Holy Week that the resurrection of Christ was preceded by unspeakable suffering. On the other hand, if our wounds, physical and psychological, have shaped who we are, both in suffering and redemption, why would we want to forget them? For like the wounds of Jesus, they are also reminders of forgiveness, grace, and transformation. If we believe that our wounds are made glorious in this life and the next, then it not only changes the way we understand ourselves but the way we relate to others in their woundedness. We realize that rather than avoiding discussion about their scarred pasts, we can invite them to tell their story through it and, by grace, to begin to witness with them the redemption of that story.

Here is the way Henri Nouwen describes this process in a book addressed to ministers of healing who must also bear their own wounds, as he comments on a rabbinic story of the Messiah as one who binds his own wounds while he awaits the moment when others will need him:

> Jesus has given this story a new fullness by making his own broken body the way to health, to liberation and new life. Thus like Jesus, he who proclaims liberation is called not only to care for his own wounds and the wounds of others, but also to make his wounds in to a major source of his healing power.[5]

In Holy Communion, the church proclaims the broken body of Jesus "the way to health" every time we celebrate this sacrament. But Nouwen suggests that followers of Jesus also must understand that our broken bodies can speak love and healing to the world's brokenness. This is particularly important in our times, when through plastic surgery, drug therapies, positive thinking, prosperity gospels, and genetic engineering, we want to cover up, deny, and therefore be ashamed of the scars that mark us for life, for time, and for eternity. Jesus invites us, like he invited Thomas, to put our hands in his wounds, to accept them as our own, that we might invite him to touch our wounds and allow him to transform them into living symbols of grace.

## Questions

1. Do you have one or more scars that reveal and remember significant episodes in your life?

2. Why do you think the glorified body of Jesus retained his scars? Will our glorified bodies reveal our scars?

3. Are you able, like Thomas, to bring your doubts to Jesus and accept his invitation to touch him?

4. Is it easier to see in others, rather than ourselves, the scarred glory of our Jesus-redeemed humanity?

5. Like Jesus, whose scars redeem the world, how can others see in our scars redemption and hope?

# 14

## Feasting with Jesus

### *Learning to Eat Between Meals*

The love ethic that pervades the ideology of African-American churches is constantly understood and reaffirmed in the exchanges of food and the celebration of church events with grand meals. This love and this hospitality remind the congregation that they are pilgrims and strangers and that as they feed somebody one day, they may stand in need on another.

Jualynne Dodson and Cheryl Townsend Gilkes[1]

Jesus attempts to show the fickle nature of the people who reject John the Baptist, who "came neither eating bread nor drinking wine," and who then reject Jesus, because "the Son of Man came eating and drinking, and you say, 'Here is a glutton and a drunkard, a friend of tax collectors and "sinners"'"(Luke 7:33–34). He knew what people said behind his back, whispered among themselves as they pretended to listen to his teaching, and occasionally shouted to his face when he aroused their anger.

Among the many ways in which Jesus was not what they or we would have expected, his attitude toward food and feasting and his joy in both—shared with followers, sinners, and even enemies—is shocking. He was never far from food and feasting, and both food and feasting were at the heart of his message and ministry. Let's catalogue in no particular order some of these events and encounters around food: the wedding at Cana, the feeding of five thousand, the feeding of four thousand, his meal with Simon Peter's mother-in-law after healing her, eating a feast with Matthew after calling him to be a disciple, eating with Zacchaeus, dining with Simon the Pharisee, dining twice with Martha and Mary, the Last Supper, supping with the two men in Emmaus, and cooking breakfast for Peter and his cohorts. This is not the picture of an ascetic rabbi or a self-abasing guru. Jesus enjoyed food, drink, and those he shared them with, not only during his ministry before the crucifixion but, even more shocking, after the resurrection. While most of the post-resurrection events described by the Gospel writers are snapshots of his activity after being raised from the dead and before he ascended to the Father, two events—his dining with the bewildered men in Emmaus and his breakfast with the disciples—are described at some length, and we will reflect on them a bit later.

## Created to Eat

So why conclude a book on the humanity of Jesus by discussing food and feasting? As I have suggested above, food and feasting were crucial to the life and ministry of Jesus. His last act before his death was to transform the last Passover meal into the first Holy Communion, on which the church has feasted for two thousand years. We are promised that when he returns to fulfill his kingdom, the first great event will be the Marriage Feast of the Lamb. If feasting and food are that important to the Triune God, then we cannot ignore them in understanding the humanity of Jesus and, through him, our humanity.

Secondly, food reminds us several times a day of our humanity, at several levels. Physically, we finite creatures need food to sustain our bodies and to boost our energy. In this need, if we care to pay attention, we know our lives are fragile and contingent upon the rest of creation. We also find in food a fulfilling of our hungry souls, whether in the healthy sharing, serving, and laughter around a communal table or in the lonely gluttony that simulates the same while snacking alone in front of a television. In food and feasting there is a longing of the spirit, whether in remembering the smell and taste of the stew that Mother simmered all day on the stove or lingering over dessert and coffee while celebrating the anniversary of good friends.

## Bingeing and Starving

Certainly, we also see the perversion of these good gifts of food and drink. So much of humanity still dies from starvation, while too many of us die from gluttony. I think, on the one hand, of Willy, a black man I met when he was working for my father's construction company. One day, sitting in the shade over lunch, we got into a conversation about our favorite foods. Willy said his was chocolate cake. He then told me of growing up poor in rural Louisiana and how, when his family was desperate, they ate corncrib rats. I looked at him in disbelief. He explained to me that, while not their meat of choice, these were not filthy city rats. They had been fattened, like cattle, on the corn stored in the barns. He quickly added that when he left Louisiana and corncrib rats forever, fleeing north to Evansville, Indiana, the first thing he did with his first paycheck was to buy a whole chocolate cake and eat it by himself at one sitting. That was a feast!

On the other hand, I think of the adolescent girls from privileged homes who were students at the prep school where I worked. I was stunned the day the school nurse talked about keeping juices and healthy snacks in the refrigerator of the clinic. A shocking number of these young women were coming to school hungry, from homes with industrial-sized kitchens, pantries and refrigerators packed with a cornucopia of foods to indulge every appetite. They were starving themselves to death so that they might appear acceptable to a culture that worships thin bodies. Here we were in a wealthy private Christian school running a free breakfast and lunch program, in much the same way our inner-city public school counterparts were doing for their hungry children. Could it be that we have replaced the Christian traditions of enjoying food in the public ceremonies of feasting and fasting with the secularized and secretive practices of bingeing and purging? How do we recover the healthy, wholesome, and joyful experience of food and feasting that Jesus lived and taught?

### Fasting and Feasting

Consider with me four events when Jesus shows how important and redemptive food and feasting can be in our lives, as they were in his life: the wedding at Cana, the Last Supper, the meal in Emmaus, and breakfast on the beach. Before we consider these, I should briefly comment on the meaning and importance of fasting in the life of Jesus and in the life of his followers. The only clear example we have of Jesus fasting is during his forty days in the wilderness, when Satan tempted him. We can infer from other incidents in his life, however, such as his preaching so long that he and the disciples forgot to allow for the crowd's need to eat or his withdrawing to the hills to pray for extended periods, that he fasted or at least skipped meals for the sake of urgent ministry and prayer. There certainly is a place for fasting in the lives of Christians; Jesus taught his disciples that after he was gone, they should expect to fast and pray.

For a majority of Christians in the history of the church, fasting has been part of the church calendar that encourages us to limit our normal indulgence of certain foods preceding both Christmas and Easter. For some of us evangelicals these traditions feel too regimented and legalistic. But many of us are coming to appreciate the importance of fasting as well as feasting. Indeed, Dorothy Bass asserts that there is among Protestants a "growing awareness that without a fast, it is hard to recognize a feast."[2] Christian thinkers such as Richard Foster, in his book *Celebration of Discipline*, not only make convincing biblical arguments for fasting but also give practical advice for how we can fast wisely. I would add that the feast, as understood in Scripture, is also a discipline, not an orgy of gluttony. The preparation, presentation, and pacing of the meal is skillful, beautiful, and moderated. For the feast is not a meal on the run or a chance to chat with friends over good food. David Ford describes it as "beyond physical or social necessity, and, like the people who celebrate it, it is an end in itself. . . . But an open end, 'with no end but delight.'"[3] Fasting, on the other hand, is not an end in itself, and there is no hint in Scripture and the teachings of Jesus that fasting will be practiced in our resurrected lives.

### Marriage Feasts

Much has rightly been made of the fact that Jesus's first recorded miracle was turning water into wine, which I discussed in an early chapter on the relationship between Jesus and his mother. Now I want to reflect with you about why a wedding feast might be the stage for his first recorded miracle. From a Jewish perspective, the answer seems obvious. Throughout the Old Testament God's relationship with Israel is described as that of a bridegroom to his bride. Whatever God's love is like in human terms, the Jewish prophets tell us that it is very like the love of a husband for his wife, even when that wife has been unfaithful. New Testament writers, most of whom were Jewish, take up this theme, from Paul's admonition "husbands, love your wives, just as Christ loved the church" (Eph. 5:25) to John's vision of the marriage feast that will inaugurate the eternal kingdom (Rev. 19:7–10).

Whether or not we know and believe the biblical witness, most of us know culturally that marriage should be celebrated over a feast. For when a couple marries, whether or not they think about it, they are marrying worlds: cultures, classes, races, families, and so forth. Families are being reconfigured forever. Not only have "two become one flesh," but also two whole traditions, often in the modern world two very different traditions, are being transformed into a new thing. So it is good and right that bride and groom heighten and extend the beauty and importance of this joining by way of feasting together. Even choosing the menu symbolizes this, as those who plan the wedding feast ponder the foods most loved by each family, as well as food and drink that are forbidden by conviction or questions of health.

As Jews and Christians, moreover, we plan and celebrate these sacred events in the presence of the God who created humanity, male and female, who blessed them to enjoy each other and embrace in their love their children, their parents, their friends, strangers, and the whole community. Indeed, according to Paul, speaking about husbands and wives loving each other like Christ loves the church, finally he is "talking about Christ and the church" (Eph. 5:32). So the celebration of the good gifts of sexuality and marriage with family and friends in the presence of God is a celebration of God's blessing in creating us in his image, male and female, and of God redeeming us in Christ, to love each other like he loves his people. Jesus knew that such a festival of love deserves the best wine and plenty of it. Jesus, through whom all things were created, celebrated all good things in that bounty of creation, which is the feast.

## Feeding Grief, Feasting Hope

By contrast, Jesus also teaches us how to share our griefs and suffering at a common table. The Passover meal that Jesus shared with his disciples on the night that he was betrayed is for Jews the remembering of suffering and grief transformed by God on the night before they began their march from slavery. Common sense would tell us that if you are about to begin a long journey in flight from vicious oppressors, you pack a suitcase and a bag lunch and flee for all you are worth. But God told Moses to tell the people to linger over one more meal, full of bitter and strange flavors, but a meal nonetheless. For they were not runaway slaves; they were liberated children of the King of Kings. And they were not to get the memories of Egypt behind them as soon as possible and move on; they were to remember Egypt and God's grace to them, sitting down annually at the Feast of the Passover, to reenact and remember whose they were and how far they had come. So, Jesus, about to be arrested, tortured, and executed, chose this meal as his last supper with his disciples before his crucifixion, so that they could linger over food, bread and wine, to heighten and dignify the last hours of their relationship and to transform that last supper into the first communion. This feast continues today as we share in his suffering through bread and wine and look forward to eating with him someday at the marriage feast.

God prepared a table before them in the presence of their enemies, especially that last great enemy—death. Food is good, even when the taste of fear and death seem to overwhelm its goodness. This is why we bring food to grieving families and eat our griefs after wakes and funerals. Food affirms life and expresses hope. Jesus teaches us how to eat our griefs and feed our hopes.

**Feeding Our Spirit**

We understand that when the Word became flesh, when God in Jesus became fully human, food would have its place in his life. We have learned that the place of food and feasting in the life of Jesus was pervasive, important, and pleasurable. But we might dismiss all of this talk of marriage feasts in the future kingdom as so much poetic language—word pictures, if you will—that enables us finite human beings to understand something of an infinite God. However, when the resurrected Jesus eats dinner and prepares and eats breakfast, we are forced to dismiss our notion of "spiritual food," whatever that might be. So when Luke tells us of Jesus walking with two despairing disciples back to their village, he certainly describes spiritual things. Jesus listens to these two grieving and confused men, who are shocked at and even critical of him for being the "only one living in Jerusalem" who has not heard of the tragic horrors of the last three days. After one of them describes to him the suffering and death he has so recently experienced, Jesus calls them foolish and slow of heart that they do not believe what the prophets have said concerning him. He then explains all of these events and himself in light of the Scriptures. The only problem is that they still don't recognize that Jesus is talking about himself. All this teaching does not bring recognition. Not until Jesus accepts their invitation to supper and breaks bread in their presence do they realize that he is their Lord.

### Revealing Ourselves

What is it about breaking bread together that enables us to recognize in each other what we were once unable to see? Is it that eating a meal reveals our common humanity, our mutual need of food? We can hide that common humanity in our offices, our cars, our meetings, and our private homes. But when we invite someone into our homes, we reveal an intimate glimpse of ourselves through our choices of food and furnishings, what hangs on our walls, and even the way we eat. Admittedly, we can also use such occasions to hide ourselves.

When I served as an assistant dean of students at a university, I came to know the food service director. One day we were discussing the VIP meals he served in the upscale and exclusive dining room. He said that the most important rules in serving meals to VIPs is that the presentation should be beautiful, and no food, such as peas or spinach, should be served that might roll off the fork or get stuck in the teeth and embarrass any of those dining. In other words, the meal should reveal nothing about those eating it. A real meal, such as Jesus shared with these two friends, reveals our appetites, our manners, how relaxed or formal we are, as well as what topics we enjoy discussing and which foods beckon us to ask for seconds.

This is also true for families, many of whom seldom eat together, partially because busy working mothers do not cook. Family meals, especially the evening meal, have been the traditional time to catch up on each other's lives, to process the experiences of the day, to discuss what the kids are studying or the projects that occupy Mom and Dad at work. A study was done some years ago in one major city, attempting to find out what the best students had in common. They concluded that the only two commonalities among these students were that they came from two-parent families with no divorce and that they ate dinner together almost every evening. I doubt that any of these families ate dinner together because they wanted to increase their children's grades or SATs. They did so because they loved each other, because they all needed to eat, because their home was a place of peace, and because they cared to know about each other's lives, thoughts, and feelings.

Just as Jesus revealed more to his friends in the breaking of the bread than in his brilliant and wise revelation of himself from Scripture, so we recognize each other over meals in ways that mere words and chance meetings cannot reveal. Sharing a meal nurtures human recognition.

### Breaking Bread and Broken Relationships

Finally, Jesus's breakfast on the beach with Peter and the other disciples reveals the reconciling power of the shared meal. Peter and the others had seen and talked with the risen Lord, but for Peter there was unresolved guilt and tension with Jesus. Peter had denied the Lord three times, despite his protests that he would never desert Jesus.

179

Probably discouraged by his moral failure, Peter did what many of us do; he went back to what he knew best, to where it all began—fishing. As you recall, they catch nothing that night until Jesus, whom they do not recognize, calls from the shore, "Throw your nets on the other side of the boat." They obey, and the nets overflow with fish. Then Peter knows who this is, and he wades to shore, where Jesus prepares a breakfast of fresh fish for his friends. No one knows what to say, even though they finally recognize him. Jesus simply eats with them, after which he turns to Peter and asks once, twice, three times: "Simon, do you love me?" Peter, with growing frustration at the repetition, affirms his love of Jesus, and Jesus confirms Peter's pastoral calling to "feed my sheep."

In considering this and other important theological insights in this splendid story, we should not miss the point that this reconciliation happened over a meal. Jesus, who created all sources of food and the human beings who are nourished by it, knew that it was best to broach reconciliation with Peter over a meal. It is often the case that the hard conversations between a husband and wife, parent and child, and colleagues at work are best shared over a meal, if our goal is reconciliation. Somehow, we are more apt to treat each other with kindness and good manners when we prepare a meal for them, pass the bread to them, and share a mutual nurturing of our bodies. On the other hand, if we prefer to nurture our hurt and anger, or in Peter's case our guilt and shame, we will refuse to eat with the person with whom we have a conflicted relationship. We stay in our bedroom and lock the door, we find excuses not to accept the invitation to lunch, or we sit sulking at the table, refusing to eat or talk. If we are unwilling to forgive or be forgiven, it is probably a good thing that we refuse to share a meal. Is this not part of the reason that Paul warns us not to participate in the Lord's Supper if we do not come to that table prepared to seek and accept forgiveness (1 Cor. 11:26–29)?

## Abusing Food

The communion meal reminds us that we live in the meantime, in a fallen world between the Last Supper and the marriage feast. In such a world, we often pervert the good gifts of God to uses for which he never intended them. Gluttony, whether that of Jabba the Hutt or of a bulimic teenager, is a deadly sin, against God, his creation, and our own bodies. I wrestle with this, as do so many others. I was fat growing up, until I entered high school, although I was told that I was merely husky. Our family, like so many others, not only enjoyed food, we also indulged in food, escaped through food, and used it as a substitute for healthy exercise and healthy relationships. I saw myself as fat Danny, even after losing weight and being in pretty good shape most of my adult life. Now that I am middle aged, I once again fight that tendency to eat out of proportion to a healthy appetite, preferring snacks, meals on the run, and comfort food. This is the plague of our affluent world where foods once not available to royalty can be pulled off the shelves of countless supermarkets or ordered up from the bloat of restaurants and fast-food joints that compete to consume us.

While gluttony is not the worst of sins, for our contemporary culture it is one of the most pervasive. For example, a friend of mine who teaches English at a prep school told me of her experience teaching Dante's *Inferno*, the story of one man's journey through hell. The levels of hell are marked by specific sins ranging from the least—lust and gluttony—to the worst—anger and pride. As you descend deeper in hell, there are liars, thieves, murderers, and those in the pit of hell, like Judas, who betrayed sacred trusts. When my friend asked her students what they honestly felt is the worst sin, they agreed that gluttony was, since they could think of nothing worse than to be fat. In a growingly secular world, where we do not believe much in the notion of sin, Os Guinness points out, "Ironically, the word 'sinful' is playfully applied to eating dessert more readily than to any other behaviors or attitudes in contemporary English."[4] We, as a culture, have cultivated a perverse relationship with food.

### The Host of the Universe

The answer to the vicious cycle of bingeing and dieting is to cultivate an attitude toward food and feasting that follows Jesus. This attitude understands the joy and discipline of feasting, as David Ford describes it:

> Hospitality is a complex matter. There are decisions about guests, menu, time and place, the work of providing and preparing a room and food and drink, and the actual performance of hosting or being entertained, with perhaps music, dancing, games, or other entertainment as well as conversation. It amounts to an extraordinary coordination

and interweaving of elements. . . . To have a vision of the feast of the Kingdom of God and to want to have foretastes of it now is, therefore, to be concerned for many things and people coming together. Perhaps the biggest vision of all is given in one verse of the letter to the Ephesians, which speaks of God having "a plan for the fullness of time, to unite [unify, recapitulate, consummate] all things in him, things in heaven and on earth" (Eph. 1:10).[5]

Ford goes on to say, "That is a stupendous picture of Jesus Christ as the host of the universe, entertaining everything and everyone."[6] In Jesus, we rediscover the joy in eating and the glory in feasting, even in a fallen world. He reveals this joy in church homecoming potlucks, coffee and snacks in the fellowship hall, Christmas dinners with extended family, serving and eating Thanksgiving meals with the homeless, lingering over coffee with a friend, and of course in Holy Communion—whether grape juice and crackers served in the pew or wine and wafers served at the rail—in which we are foretasting in his humanity, and in our own, the feast being prepared by "the host of the universe."

If we can understand that Jesus serves as potential host to all our eating, whether everyday meals or celebratory feasts, we can begin to enjoy our food as the sacred yet fully human act of eating between meals. By this I mean that our lives and the history of the church are lived between the Last Supper and the Marriage Feast of the Lamb. Experienced this way, all our enjoyment of food in the meantime is learning to allow Jesus's presence to grace every act of eating between these two great meals.

## Questions

1. Why do you suspect that food and feasting were so central to Jesus's life and ministry?
2. How has food functioned in your life?
3. Have you experienced healthy models of careful preparation and joyful feasting? If so, what makes them memorable to you?
4. What part does communion play in your worship of and remembering Jesus?
5. From the four examples of Jesus sharing himself over meals, in what ways can you imagine enjoying food with family, friends, or strangers as a ministry of love and redemption?

# Notes

## Introduction

1. J. B. Phillips, *Ring of Truth* (New York: Macmillan, 1967), 87.

## Chapter 1 Manger Wetter

1. Stephen Mahan, "Manger Wetter," used by permission.
2. John Donne, "Annunciation," *The Complete Poetry and Selected Prose of John Donne*, edited with introduction by Charles M. Coffin (New York: Modern Library, 1952), 231.
3. "The Mwindo Epic," *African Folktales*, selected and retold by Roger D. Abrahams (New York: Pantheon Books, 1983), 240ff.
4. Peter Drucker, *The Effective Executive* (New York: Harper Collins, 1996), 75.
5. C. S. Lewis, *A Preface to Paradise Lost* (London: Oxford University Press, 1974), 94–103.
6. Peter Senge, *The Fifth Discipline* (New York: Doubleday, 1990), 17–26.
7. James Fowler, *Becoming Adult, Becoming Christian* (San Francisco: Jossey-Bass, 2000), 84.

## Chapter 2 Longing to Belong

1. Gerard Manley Hopkins, "God's Grandeur," *Gerard Manley Hopkins: Poems and Prose*, selected and edited by W. H. Gardner (London: Penguin Books, 1963), 27.

## Chapter 3 Mother's Guilt

1. Erma Bombeck, "When your mother asks . . ." (www.inspirationalquotes4U.com/bombeckquotes).

## Chapter 4 The Problem of Authority

1. Dorothy L. Sayers, *The Mind of the Maker* (San Francisco: Harper, 1987), 87–88.
2. Donald Cowan, "The Tough Style," *Classic Texts and the Nature of Authority* (Dallas: The Dallas Institute Publications, 1993), 100–106.
3. Dorothy Sayers, "The Human-Not-Quite-Human," *Unpopular Opinions* (London: Victor Gollancz Ltd., 1946), 118–19.
4. Ibid., 121–22.
5. Ibid.

## Chapter 5 The Failures of Jesus

1. Parker Palmer, *The Courage to Teach* (San Francisco: Jossey-Bass, 1998), 37.
2. Fowler, *Becoming Adult, Becoming Christian*, 84.

## Chapter 6 In Need of Friends

1. C. S. Lewis, *The Four Loves* (New York: Harcourt Brace Jovanovich, 1960), 103.
2. Robert Coles, *The Privileged Ones* (Boston: An Atlantic Monthly Press Book, 1977), 413–56.
3. Lewis, *The Four Loves*, 87.
4. Ibid.
5. Ibid., 91.

## Chapter 7 The Dysfunctions of Jesus's Family

1. Leo Tolstoy, *Anna Karenina*, translated by Louise and Aylmer Maude (New York: W. W. Norton & Company, 1970), 1.

2. Christopher Lasch, *Haven in a Heartless World: The Family Besieged* (New York: Basic Books, 1977), xiii.

3. C. S. Lewis, *The Great Divorce* (San Francisco: Harper, 1973), 97–104.

### Chapter 8 Jesus and Sex

1. Leo Steinberg, *The Sexuality of Christ in Renaissance Art and in Modern Oblivion* (Chicago: University of Chicago Press, 1983), 64.

2. C. S. Lewis, *Mere Christianity* (New York: Macmillan Publishing Company, 1960), 46.

3. Steinberg, *The Sexuality of Christ in Renaissance Art and in Modern Oblivion*, 21, n20.

### Chapter 9 Good and Angry

1. Anglican Bishop Jeremy Taylor, as quoted in *Wounds Not Healed by Time* by Solomon Schimmel (Oxford: Oxford University Press, 2002), 54.

2. Abraham Heschel, *The Prophets*, vol. 2 (Peabody: Prince Press, 2001), 80.

3. Martin Luther King Jr., *Letter from Birmingham Jail* (San Francisco: Harper, 1994), 1.

### Chapter 10 When Jesus Questioned the Father

1. William Edgar, "Shadow," *It Was Good Making Art to the Glory of God*, edited by Ned Bustard (Baltimore: Square Halo Press, 2006), 239.

2. Aleksandr Solzhenitsyn, *The First Circle* (New York: Bantam Books, 1969), 1–6.

### Chapter 11 Extreme Jesus

1. F. Scott Fitzgerald, *The Great Gatsby* (New York: Charles Scribner's Sons, 1925), 1.

### Chapter 12 How Should Christians Die?

1. T. S. Eliot, "The Wasteland," *T. S. Eliot: The Complete Poems and Plays 1909–1950* (New York: Harcourt, Brace & World), 39.

2. C. S. Lewis, *Essays Presented to Charles Williams* (Grand Rapids: William B. Eerdmans Publishing Company, 1966), xiv.

3. e. e. cummings, "When God Lets My Body Be," *The American Tradition in Literature* (New York: W. W. Norton, 1967), 1573.

4. Bill Joy, "Why the Future Doesn't Need Us," *Wired* 8, no. 4 (April 2000): 47–48.

5. Ibid., 48.

6. Ibid.

### Chapter 13  Scarred for Life

1. Homer, *The Odyssey*, translated by Robert Fitzgerald (Garden City: Doubleday, 1961), 339.

2. N. T. Wright, *The Challenge of Jesus* (Downers Grove: InterVarsity Press, 1999), 134.

3. "The Parable of the Liberal Education," an address by Dr. Walter Hansen given at Gordon College in August 2006.

4. C. S. Lewis, *The Weight of Glory and Other Addresses* (San Francisco: HarperCollins, 2001), 46.

5. Henri Nouwen, *The Wounded Healer* (New York: Doubleday, 1972), 82–83.

### Chapter 14  Feasting with Jesus

1. Jualynne Dodson and Cheryl Townsend Gilkes, "There's Nothing Like Church Food," *Journal of the American Academy of Religion* 63, no. 3 (Fall 1995): 520–21.

2. Dorothy C. Bass, *Receiving the Day* (San Francisco: Jossey-Bass, 2000), 105.

3. David F. Ford, *The Shape of Living* (Grand Rapids: Baker Books, 1997), 185.

4. *Steering Through Chaos*, compiled by Os Guinness and edited by Virginia Mooney (Colorado Springs: NavPress, 2000), 212.

5. Ford, *The Shape of Living*, 188.

6. Ibid.

**Dan Russ** (PhD, University of Dallas) is the director of the Center for Christian Studies at Gordon College. He has been a Young Life leader and a high school teacher, and he has taught the Bible and classical literature to business professionals, city planners, and attorneys, as well as to college and graduate students in seminars on moral values and vision. Russ lives in Danvers, Massachusetts, with his wife, Kathy.